All We Need
Is a
Happy Ending

Diane Farley's true story of life, love,
and Alzheimer's disease.

Renae Farley

All We Need Is a Happy Ending

Diane Farley's true story of life, love,
and Alzheimer's disease

Published by
Keep The Peace Publishing

For publishing and distribution inquires contact:
Keep The Peace Publishing
6965 El Camino Real #105
PMB 486
Carlsbad, CA 92009
www.RenaeFarley.com

Printed in the United States of America

ISBN-13: 978-1517221775
ISBN-10: 1517221773

Library of Congress Control Number 2013950129

Cover design by Drew Bailey

Photos of Diane Farley courtesy of Renae Farley

Renae Farley's author photo by Blue Flair Photography

Dedication

In memory of my beautiful sister
and in gratitude for my loving husband.

Contents

Love recognizes no barriers.
It jumps hurdles, leaps fences, penetrates walls
to arrive at its destination full of hope.

Maya Angelou

Introduction

This is a true story, but the names of the physicians involved have been changed to protect their privacy.

This story began before I knew I was in it, before any of us knew we were in it. It was a journey, our journey, for which there was no preparation. This is the story of our family's experience with early-onset Alzheimer's disease.

Many people will experience Alzheimer's disease, but only some will fall into the early-onset category, meaning they have symptoms before age 65. Early onset can begin as early as the 40s. I hope that by learning what we went through with my sister, you will become aware of some of the warning signs and can provide informed support to your loved ones.

According to the Alzheimer's Association, every 58 seconds, someone in the U.S. develops Alzheimer's disease. The latest estimates show that 5.4 million Americans are living with this tragic disease. In San Diego, where we live,

The First Signs

53,000 people have Alzheimer's disease, and more than 100,000 people care for them. I've been a runner for 42 years. I do my best thinking when I'm out on my beach runs, and I've been doing that three times a week for the past seven years. I run five miles along the beautiful cliffs of Carlsbad, California—doing my running meditations and healing requests, offering my prayers, and solving problems related to both my work and my personal life. This routine works more often than not and helps me find peace. I think about everything I have to be grateful for on the first half of my run, and then I visualize what I want in the future on the last half.

On one of these runs, I visualized myself walking hand in hand with my divine male companion through our vineyard in Tuscany, somewhat like Meg Ryan and Kevin Klein in my all-time favorite movie, "French Kiss." Because I adore Italy, my own "movie" takes place there instead of France.

Suddenly, my visualization was interrupted with a new element. For me to be living in Italy, I had to make sure that my sister, Diane, was living happily somewhere, too. I started visualizing her finding her true soul mate and living in Del Mar, her ideal city, where she'd never have to worry about anything again.

How could we both afford to realize these visualizations and live happily ever after? Several ideas ran through my mind, but there was one I kept coming back to: perhaps we could tell Diane's story. I'd write it, because she no longer could, and we'd use the proceeds to make our dreams come true! I visualized our book on the New York Times' bestseller list. I believe everyone loves a book with a happy ending. What better happy ending than being able to beat and walk away from a horrible disease?

I was raised with the belief that I can do anything I set my mind to, thanks to my dad, Bud. I'd never written anything in my life, nor had I ever taken a writing class, but that didn't stop me. I was on a mission with a great purpose.

This story began on St. Patrick's Day 2004. My sister Diane, my best buddy, was 50 at the time and had invited my dad and me over for her traditional meal of corned beef and cabbage. Diane loved to cook and was very good in the kitchen. She was always neatly dressed, so I was a little surprised when she answered the door in a lounge dress with no bra and no makeup. I figured maybe she'd lost track of time and didn't realize we'd be there so soon.

After a wonderful meal, we sat down to play a simple game of Phase 10. We'd played this card game for years and Diane often won, but she was having a very difficult time concentrating and figuring out the cards that night. We poked fun at her as she kept telling us she was suffering from "brain fogs" because she was going through menopause. She'd been experiencing hot flashes the entire evening, which we also teased her about, all in good fun because that's just how my family is.

Diane had been telling me about these fogs for some time, but I'd never seen her acting as totally confused as she was that night. It was frightening, because she couldn't put the cards together in simple sets or runs of four. She was actually holding her cards fanned backward. She asked us to count her cards for scoring purposes at the end of each hand. Something wasn't right, but I just assumed it was the result of menopause, as Diane said she'd been reading about in all her magazines.

Diane was my favorite sister. We'd joke about this because she was my only sister, and we were as different as night and day. Diane was 5'2" with long red curly hair, very white skin with lots of red freckles, full figured, a bit overweight, and very feminine. She was very pretty but didn't like to attract attention to herself, so she dressed down and wore minimal makeup; she just couldn't be bothered with primping. She was shy around strangers, but around those she knew she was a real comedian and you couldn't get a word in edgewise when she started to talk.

I was always envious of Diane's dry wit. Even at work, she kept the women in her office laughing. She hated to work out or sweat and was very content to sit around on weekends and watch TV or a good movie for the third time; read magazines, including her favorite, Martha Stewart Living; or cook. She was definitely a homebody and loved to garden in her petite yard. Mellow was the perfect word to describe Diane. She seemed content with her life except in one important area: she hated her job!

I'm 5'7", very lean with short blond hair, tan, and very athletic and have always been a tomboy. I'm always reading personal development books or listening to educational tapes. I love to travel and have been to 18 countries. I've run my own interior design business for 28 years and love what I do. I've been called somewhat of a perfectionist and have a very difficult time just sitting around. You can see that Diane and I were definitely different, but we loved doing many of the same things as well. She was my best buddy.

In mid-July 2004, I called to leave a message on Diane's home answering machine about an event I wanted us to go to that weekend. I was surprised when she answered the phone because she should have been at work; I assumed she must be home sick. She told me she'd been suspended because she was having a hard time concentrating. Diane had a lot on her plate at that time. She was getting ready to have a hysterectomy because she was having problems with fibroids; her doctor noticed they were growing quite rapidly, to the size of a baseball. After surgery, she was going to recuperate at my house. I'd always been skeptical about doctors who think surgery is a go-to cure, but I wanted to be there for Diane.

In the meantime, Diane's employer was, as she put it, "not being very kind" to her. For more than 18 years, she'd worked at a San Diego TV and radio station in the TV traffic department, which means she was in charge of arranging all the commercials that go on the air. This job is extremely stressful because the salespeople often change things at the last minute and, if there's a mistake, it could cost the station thousands of dollars. Apparently, Diane had made one of these costly mistakes. The "powers that be" felt she was under too much stress from her upcoming surgery, so they told her to take a little time off and not return until she'd fully recovered.

Only a few months earlier, when Diane's boss was retiring, she was asked to succeed her, meaning she'd be the head of the department. I remember the whole family was together for a birthday party when she gave us the news and we all cheered her on—but she followed that announcement by saying she didn't think she'd accept the position because she didn't feel she was up for it. She didn't think she was smart enough.

This kind of talk really upset me because Diane was a very bright woman; she could do anything she set her mind to. I think she was already having some issues with her memory and was having difficulty learning new things. A few months earlier, she'd been sent to Colorado for instruction on her company's new computer system and it was a real struggle for her. I think this is when she started losing confidence.

Diane told me she wanted to see a Chinese doctor, Dr. Chang, who specialized in holistic healing using herbs. A friend at work had taken his young son to see this doctor because the boy was having frequent seizures. The little boy even had brain surgery, but to no avail. Traditional medicine was unable to cure him, but after several visits to this doctor, his seizures had stopped. Diane was hopeful he could give her something to clear up her brain fogs.

Diane was always interested in reading medical dictionaries. She had a huge one she referenced whenever she or anyone she knew had a medical issue. Later, when she had her own computer, she'd read about medicine on the Internet. When our dad was told he had high blood pressure, she researched the topic and provided him with all the ways to control it with food and diet instead of taking traditional medication.

I decided to take Diane to see Dr. Chang because she needed a little help communicating, and I was very curious to learn more about this type of medicine myself. A young woman showed us to the exam room and told Diane to sit in a chair. We were a bit surprised—no undressing, no white paper gown? Dr. Chang came in, introduced himself, and said, "Stick out your tongue." He grabbed Diane's tongue with a piece of gauze, looked underneath it, and then turned it to the right and left. He said everything in the body was represented in the tongue and he could tell what was wrong with most people just by analyzing it.

After the tongue examination, the doctor walked us out to the reception desk, which was in front of several shelves of large clear glass bottles, an apothecary of sorts that contained lots of really strange looking herbs and roots. He laid out a piece of blue paper, put a little bit of several of these gnarly things in the middle of it, and wrapped them up. He told Diane to make tea using this herb concoction and drink it twice a day. He also changed her diet a bit and put some restrictions on her eating habits. We'd have to wait and see how she did after following this new regimen for a few weeks.

During this time, we had a large family wedding and all our friends and family who talked to Diane could see a significant change in her. Many of them hadn't seen her in some time, and they noticed right away that she seemed very confused. They were very worried about her and asked me if I could start helping her.

That week, I took over all Diane's correspondence with the human resources people at the TV station and completed all the paperwork necessary for her to collect short-term disability while she was off work for six weeks for her surgery and recovery. She apparently had been told she had to fill out all this paperwork weeks earlier but hadn't done it yet. I don't think she could.

I also received advice from Jack, our "plastic" brother-in-law, as he likes to be called. Jack is my brother's brother-in-law, but he is considered family because we have all been together for 25 years. Jack suggested that I consult with his attorney, who specialized in medical law. We were just being cautious at this point to make sure Diane was being protected if the TV station was going to fire her because of her situation. We set up a meeting with the attorney and he gave us a list of everything we needed to do. Thank goodness for him, because we were clueless. Remember, I'm an interior designer, an artist; what did I know about any of this? I didn't know it at the time, but I was about to become very familiar very fast.

Good News

We had some good news the day before Diane's surgery when she went into the hospital for her pre-op workup. The fibroids had substantially shrunk, they were practically nonexistent, and the surgery was not necessary! I was thrilled she didn't have to go through that ordeal.

At Diane's next appointment with Dr. Chang, we told him her surgery had been canceled. He said she had never needed surgery, because fibroids would eventually shrink and disappear without the need for an invasive procedure. The herb tea hadn't helped with the brain fogs, but it had quickly shrunk the fibroids. We were elated; it was a wonderful and unexpected side effect.

Now, however, Diane was supposed to go back to work, and she was in no condition to do that. She hadn't improved mentally and was becoming progressively worse. I was able to get her primary doctor to allow her to take six weeks of disability anyway until we could figure out what was going on in that sweet little brain of hers.

In mid-August, the human resources people said that before Diane could go on short-term disability, she'd have to be seen by a doctor. The one they sent us to was a neurologist, Dr. Parkins, who tapped Diane's knees and elbows and did a few other tests that took about two minutes. He then asked Diane a few questions about work and she just burst out, "I don't ever want to work behind a desk again!"

Dr. Parkins looked at her for a moment, made a quick note, and sent us on our way. His conclusion was that Diane was suffering from stress. He recommended she see a psychiatrist and have a neuropsychological evaluation. I was very unimpressed with Dr. Parkins and felt he jumped to a conclusion because of Diane's statement about work.

What follows is a quote from the Alzheimer's Association's weekly newsletter, About.com. You'll see these kinds of quotations throughout the book where they pertain to what was happening in Diane's progression with the disease.

> Researchers found, through work with mice, that chronic emotional stress seems to affect the health of the brain and those exposed to repeated stress began to develop some of the neurofibrillary tangles of tau protein that are characteristic of the human brain as Alzheimer's develops.—About.com, April 2012

One thing Dr. Parkins said did make sense to me. He equated Diane's position with that of an air traffic controller. He said, "You can only put a brain under that kind of stress for so long and then it will short out." Diane worked under this stress 8 hours a day for 18 years. I remember she especially hated the political season, because her life at work became even worse with all the political commercials constantly being changed and moved around at the last minute.

Diane was very unhappy working behind a computer and told me every time I saw her that she hated her job and wanted out. She consistently said she didn't want to work anymore. I used to tell her to be careful what she put out into the universe, as it might just give her what she asked for. I'm one of those who believe in the "law of attraction"— that is, what you think about, good or bad, will come into your life whether you want it or not.

At that time, I realized or perhaps came to believe that Diane had wished her condition upon herself so she didn't have to work at the station anymore, and she was too frightened to make the big leap of finding a new job. I remembered a saying by some wise person: The stories of your mind become the stories of your life. I believe it holds some truth.

Before any of this happened, I had many conversations with Diane about taking a day off to apply for another job. I told her she'd be hired anywhere she wanted to work. She was so cute and clever and everyone loved her, but she was too afraid even back then, when everything was fine with her health. I once told her I didn't want to hear her complain anymore until she took some action and did something about her situation. I was trying "tough love."

During this period, Diane told me what she really wanted to do. She'd been asked at the station one day to help with a voiceover for a commercial. The station managers really liked her voice, and she decided she wanted to do voiceovers for a living. It sounded great! She wouldn't have to dress up and do her hair and makeup, which would have been a perfect situation for her. She could show up, read her lines, and get compensated very well.

To help Diane with this new dream, I discovered that the local junior college had classes in voiceovers. I said I'd register and go to the classes with her if she wanted me to. Even at this time, I'd begun to realize that in her existing mental state, she really couldn't do this. We needed to keep trying to figure out what was going on in her head.

At this point, because the doctors thought Diane's problems were the result of stress and possibly work-related, she was eligible for workers' compensation. New contacts had to be made and new paperwork completed to apply for it. Thank goodness I didn't work for someone else, and I could take care of all this. I always wondered what people do if they can't get time off to help a loved one.

At the request of the station's human resources department, we were off to see another doctor, Dr. Abdul, the occupational health specialist at Sharp Rees-Stealy. He'd evaluate Diane and give his opinion on her state of mind, including whether she needed a neuropsychological evaluation. He agreed, with a little coaxing from me, that this was a necessary next step.

We were then sent to a quirky older doctor, Dr. Gerald, who was a psychiatrist. He was a real character who wore hearing aids in both ears and yelled instead of talked to us. He kept yelling "what?" every time we spoke. He talked more about himself than questioning Diane. This would prove to be true with many of the doctors we'd encounter; the egos involved were amazing. When I asked him about requesting the neuropsychological evaluation, he agreed it was the only way to really figure out what was going on with Diane. Dr. Gerald did make a statement that never left me: "She's acting like she's had a stroke."

A Miracle

Six years earlier, Diane had a pulmonary embolism and was lucky she survived. She hyperventilated one day on her lunch break and was so scared she drove herself to Green Hospital. The emergency room doctor did a quick exam and told her she had pleurisy, a lung infection. She was given some antibiotics, sent home, and told to make an appointment for a follow-up in two weeks.

That weekend we had a family birthday party and I saw Diane limping. When I asked her why, she pulled up her pant leg and showed me a huge bruise covering her whole ankle, which was very swollen. When I said she should go to the doctor right away because she didn't know how she got the bruise, she told me about the incident at Green Hospital. She said she'd ask about the bruise when she went back to check on her "pleurisy."

Before Diane's follow-up visit, we headed up to our family's mountain house in Arrowhead, something we did quite often.

It was very cold with lots of snow on the ground. I soon got cabin fever and made Diane go for a walk with me. We'd gone just a few blocks when Diane stopped in her tracks and her face literally turned the same color as the snow; I thought she was going to pass out! I took her back to the house and she sat down for a while. She was soon fine, so I just forgot all about it.

When Diane went back to the doctor the next week, she checked her out and said she saw no more signs of pleurisy. Diane then showed the doctor her ankle. The doctor immediately freaked out and admitted her to the hospital, knowing that what she'd diagnosed as pleurisy was actually a pulmonary embolism, a blood clot! She'd really blown it; her mistake could have killed Diane!

Diane was hospitalized for a day before she had a chance to call me. She left me a message that she was in the hospital but forgot to tell me which one or why! Because she didn't have a cell phone at that time, I had to sit and wait until she called me again. Once she called back, I rushed to the hospital only to find that a priest was giving her last rights! We aren't Catholic, so I didn't understand what was going on. There were machines all around Diane, and the staff were asking me to sign all kinds of paperwork about how long I wanted to keep her alive if she slipped into a coma, etc. What the hell?

The doctors were doing several tests on Diane to see where the blot clot was located in her body. They were ready to do surgery and install something below her heart, like an umbrella, that would capture the blood clot before it got there. When they did the test, however, they saw the clot had already passed through her lungs and heart and had done no damage! This was a miracle and apparently doesn't happen very often. I was told later that every year, 60,000 people die of blood clots going to the heart or have massive strokes because the blood clot makes it to the brain. Everyone was rather baffled at how this could have happened with no apparent side effects.

I have two theories. One is that Diane was admitted into the hospital on April 16th, our mother's birthday, and she was her guardian angel watching over her. Our mom took her own life when I was 19 and Diane was 22 because she lost her long battle fighting depression. I was the one who came home from school and found my mom, and it screwed me up a bit. I think my mom knew I couldn't lose Diane, too, and she stepped in that day.

My second theory is that the day I made Diane go for a walk in the mountains at that high altitude (our home was at 6,000 feet), her heart was really pumping and it forced the blood clot to pass. I told her if she'd been sitting on the sofa when that happened she might not have made it. I always joked that I'd saved her life by making her exercise.

Diane had to stay flat on her back in the hospital for close to a week, hooked up to an IV containing heparin, a blood thinner, to ensure that there were no more clots. I sat with her every day.

One afternoon, Diane's good friend from work, Pam, came to visit. Pam is a real hoot, and before long we decided to play hangman to cheer up Diane. We played the game on the nurses' white board, and when one nurse came in and saw us she was a bit ticked off and ready to kick us out. I took the nurse out in the hallway and said, "Either I can sit in there and cry with worry or we can make the best of the situation and have some fun with Diane." She left us alone after that.

The doctors thought the clot was the result of Diane's being on birth control pills and leading a sedentary life/ not exercising. Diane stayed on Coumadin, another blood thinner, for about a year after being discharged and had no further incidents.

I told Diane after "the great blood clot scare" that she'd been given a second chance at life and needed to start working out to keep her blood flowing to her brain. She hated to sweat and was not one who took easily to an exercise routine, although she would walk once in a while. Eventually I gave up trying, feeling as though I was being a real nag.

Irrational Thinking

On the last weekend of October 2004, I was asked to go to Las Vegas with two girlfriends, Jackie and Lorraine, to celebrate my birthday. Because I was born the day before Halloween, it was always my favorite holiday and a big part of my birthday celebration. Diane volunteered to stay at my house and "cat sit" my two girls, Cleo and Cinder. Diane always called them her nieces. Neither Diane nor I (or our brother, Rick) had human children, only furry ones.

Diane never planned vacations on her own because I was the only one she knew who traveled. I'd been traveling with others a lot, and she used her vacation days to hang out at my house when I was gone because I lived too far away from her job to commute each day. She loved the getaway and being around the cats; she had no pets but was a huge animal lover. In Diane's younger years, she always had cats and dogs.

Before I left for the airport, I put a black plastic cauldron full of candy by the front door and told Diane to give it out to the trick-or-treaters in case she was still there on Sunday night. When I got home late Sunday night, she was gone and the candy wasn't in the cauldron anymore but laid out very neatly on two paper plates. I was bemused; why had she done this?

The next morning I went to empty the litter box. I had one of those electronic litter boxes that automatically rakes up the litter and dumps it in a plastic container 10 minutes after the cat does her business; a lid comes down to keep the area smelling fresh. Diane had emptied the litter box numerous times, but this time she'd put the plastic tray in upside down, which was really difficult to do, and litter was everywhere.

When I called Diane to thank her for watching my girls and ask if we had any trick-or-treaters, she said, "Well, I waited around until 5:00 and no one came so I left." I said it didn't really get dark until 6:00, and they weren't going to come out before then. She replied, "I'm sure parents wouldn't let their children out after dark!" This really scared me because now she not only was having major brain fogs but also was thinking quite irrationally and doing strange things.

...the synapses start flipping off one by one...—Alz.org

It took many phone calls and written requests to get to our next step, but in November Diane was sent to be evaluated by Dr. Mendez, a neuropsychological psychologist. This step comprised a two-day written and verbal exam. It apparently cost several thousand dollars, which is why the insurance company was not real thrilled to set it up for us.

After all the waiting, I finally got to speak to Dr. Mendez and he was very nice. He said Diane's symptoms were very rare and he was convinced they weren't caused by something physical. He believed she could be suffering from a hysterical condition caused by stress in an industrial condition (her job). He said all the information he'd put into his computer the past few days had even confused the machine! He sent her to another doctor, Dr. Brinkmoor, who specialized in forensic psychiatry and psychoanalysis.

I wasn't able to sit in on Diane's sessions with either Dr. Mendez or Dr. Brinkmoor because of the personal issues that would be discussed. I didn't have her power of attorney at this time and realize now that I should have been there.

I think both these medical professionals were confused and didn't know what else to do with Diane, so they recommended she stay on workers' comp. Her prescription would be weekly sessions with a psychiatrist, and she was referred to Dr. Harper.

I went to her first session to make sure he was okay before I subjected her to him. Dr. Harper worked out of his home and seemed to be a pretty nice guy. He did talk about himself a lot the first day, which made me wonder a little. Diane went to a few more sessions on her own, and she said he talked about himself a lot and she really wasn't getting much out of it.

This doctor might have tried to keep a conversation going because Diane wasn't able to do much talking now. Her verbal skills were getting worse. In the past, she sometimes had a hard time remembering a word, which we all do from time to time, but now she couldn't even put a sentence together. She'd get very frustrated when trying to explain something to me, and I'd have to be very patient with her and tell her not to rush it, that it would come.

But the words weren't coming easily at all anymore. Because I spent so much time around Diane and usually knew what was going on with her, I became somewhat of a mind reader. I'd just keep putting words out there until she said, "Yes!"

In the meantime, Dr. Brinkmoor wanted Diane to see yet another doctor. He said he wasn't convinced about the "diagnosis"; he believed they were missing something. He was concerned that stroke had been mentioned and that Diane had had a pulmonary embolism, so he wanted to check into a few more things. He thought perhaps she was having tiny embolisms that could be shooting tiny blood clots to the brain and causing very minor strokes that were not showing up on her MRI.

I happened to be talking about Diane's situation to one of my clients while remodeling his home. He was a heart specialist, and he thought she could be suffering from patent foramen ovale, which is a hole in the heart. I went back to the insurance company to request a test to eliminate this as a possibility. These results quickly came back clear: no hole in the heart.

I have to say that dealing with insurance companies could have been such a nightmare, but I was blessed with two angels who were totally sympathetic with me and got back to me almost immediately. One of my angels, a long-term disability expert, held my hand all the way through this tunnel of paperwork and bureaucracy. The other, a workers' comp specialist, was amazingly helpful to me for the many months we worked together. There are "real" people at the end of those phone lines. I felt like we'd become friends by the time our professional relationships ended.

It probably helped that I always seemed to be in tears when talking to these women because I was so scared and frustrated. I think they went way out of their way to help me because they felt so bad for Diane and so sorry for me.

I kept reassuring Diane with every test she took that we were eliminating every possible disease. She was such a trooper. She'd been through a lot and hadn't complained once; in fact, she was just happy not to have to go to work!

My same doctor client said if he were in my shoes, he'd take Diane to Mayo Clinic and spend $10,000 or whatever it took to have the best doctors in the world look at her and figure out things once and for all. Dad was willing to do this. I suggested Diane first finish with the next few tests they wanted to do on her, and if they still hadn't come up with a conclusion, we'd fly Diane to the Mayo Clinic in Phoenix.

Bud, our dad (who Diane called Budley), was not good at dealing with any of this; he was glad I was handling all the paperwork and doctor appointments. Dad was very concerned about Diane and called me often to check on the latest development.

Our dad is the best! He's in his late 70s and only 5'6". I always wear high heels, and I love towering over him as he tells everyone I'm his little girl. He is just adorable. He has a little too much belly and his formerly beautiful full head of black hair is pretty thin, but those Paul Newman blue eyes are still working their magic and he remains a very handsome man. He has a great sense of humor and has always been there for us, no matter what.

Dad was born and raised in Jamestown, North Dakota, where he and my mom met and married. Shortly after Rick and Diane were born, my mom and dad decided to move to San Diego, following my mom's brother and his wife, Uncle Earl and Aunt Vonnie. I thank Dad often for that brave move so I could be born in America's Finest City!

Dad retired from Pearson Ford, where he was the parts manager for 47 years. Diane was his cashier for a few years when she was young. He's well respected in the community and loved by all who know him. He's never been sick a day in his life and is a hard guy to keep up with. He always seems to be off in his 37-foot motor home on another new adventure.

Dad, Diane, and I were all single for a long time. (Dad actually got "coupled up" first!) Diane and I always went out on Friday nights and then suddenly Dad wanted to tag along with us. We'd go to the movies and dinner and talk about anything, as if he was just one of the girls. Dad got to know everything about women on these nights out. He was kind of putting a damper on our meeting men, but it was cool; we felt so grateful to have a dad who was also our friend. I always felt there was a special bond between the three of us.

Dr. Brinkmoor now wanted Diane to see another specialist, Dr. Warner, who worked in neurology and nerve conduction and specialized in dementia, which was the next thing we wanted to eliminate. We walked into his office and as usual I began my story of what we'd been going through, all the doctors we'd seen, and what Diane's issues were. I did all the speaking because Diane was really unable to remember what we'd already gone through. She'd explain to each doctor that I was her voice.

This particular doctor very rudely cut me off and told Diane to get undressed; he'd be back in a few minutes to examine her. Dr. Warner did the tapping of the knees and elbows and few other tests. He ran a tool up the bottom of Diane's bare feet and her right toe turned up slightly. When we left, I was furious at what a jerk he was. I'd taken half a day off work to go to this appointment and he didn't want to hear a thing I had to say. Very poor bedside manner! By now it was mid-January 2005, 10 months and 10 doctors later. Perhaps I was getting a little frustrated, you think?

In February 2005, Dr. Brinkmoor called to warn me that Diane would be taken off workers' comp because of a report he'd just received from Dr. Warner. Dr. Brinkmoor also said Diane should stop seeing the psychiatrist; the insurance company would no longer pay him, because it thought this was now a long-term disability issue. That part didn't disappoint Diane; she didn't want to go to any more sessions with the psychiatrist anyway.

Because Dr. Warner had seen the big toe on Diane's right foot turn up and based on a few other things he noticed, he was thinking it was dementia! Dr. Brinkmoor gave me his condolences and said how sorry he was. He added that he cared for both of us and if I ever needed to talk to him, his door was always open.

What? I was freaking out! This can't be happening! What is he saying? It was not quite sinking in. I was in shock and broke into tears. I had to cancel all my client appointments that day and had no idea what to do next.

In one of those odd life coincidences, a few hours later my dad called and asked if I wanted to go to lunch. We NEVER go to lunch because I'm usually way too busy and just don't DO lunch. Plus, Dad lives 45 minutes away from me. I sobbed while telling him about the conversation I'd just had with Dr. Brinkmoor and we agreed to meet halfway, in Del Mar, for lunch.

Dad brought an article he'd seen in the Mayo Clinic newsletter, something he started subscribing to after it had been brought up as a place to take Diane. The piece was about dementia. I read it in the restaurant and started crying, because everything in it sounded just like Diane. Dad said his older sister had just been diagnosed with dementia and was doing quite well on the drug Aricept. That made two cases in our family. We also had an aunt on my mother's side who'd had dementia for many years—but both aunts were in their late 70s when they were afflicted. Diane was only 50!

Dad and I had a very long talk over lunch and then sat in his car in the parking lot for a long time, trying to wrap our minds around the whole idea. There were many tears as we talked about what we would do, where Diane would live, how she would live. It was all quite surreal. How was I going to tell her this could be a possibility?

Then I got angry! How dare this doctor call me and give me his condolences when he was not even sure! We hadn't even seen the doctor who'd give us the definite diagnosis—so I slipped back into denial mode to cope.

In the meantime, I was hanging out with Diane on one of our Friday nights in downtown San Diego's Gaslamp Quarter, which was one of our favorite things to do. Dad had a girlfriend now, so he no longer hung out with us. We stopped into a pub to have a beer when I decided I needed to tell her about the conversation I had with Dr. Brinkmoor, that he was trying to tell us she had dementia. She took it as she always took everything that came her way, with grace and no fear. We decided if she did have IT, we knew we could reverse it.

Changing Her Thought Process

Luckily, I'd been able to convince Diane to listen to some wonderful tapes called "Abraham Hicks." A good friend had given them to me years earlier, and I'd listened to them over and over again. I like what they have to say. Whether you believe in Abraham or not, it's the philosophy behind the words that connected with me.

The tapes are about a couple that learned to speak to a being from the "other side" through meditation. Abraham is the name of the being that represents all "God-like thoughts" and Hicks is the couple's last name. They offer many wonderful suggestions on how to think and live more positively—and they support the law of attraction. They believe, as I do, that what you think can affect what actually comes into your life, whether you want it or not, both good and bad, so you need to monitor your thoughts.

The stories in your mind become the stories of your life.—Author unknown

No stinkin thinkin.—Zig Ziglar

I've listened to tapes like this for most of my adult life and had asked Diane to try them several times throughout the years, but she wasn't ready to hear their message. I was listening to them in my car, as I did periodically, and asked Diane again if she'd like to listen to them. She said, "No, and I don't want you to be disappointed when they don't work for you either." I was only disappointed that I couldn't get her to open her mind to some new thinking. I was a bit hurt and got a little teary when I said, "I'll never share any of this with you again, I promise." I think she realized she'd hurt my feelings.

A few days later she called and said she'd changed her mind; she did want to listen to the tapes, and I loaned her the entire set (five tapes). Every time we talked after this, she was so excited about what she'd learned and was putting the information to use in her own thinking—just in the nick of time.

Diane had a bad habit of saying that she never wanted to work again, and similar things. I told her she'd said such things so often over the years that might be why they manifested themselves. I believe you need to be careful about how you ask for things and put them in the right context, such as "I'd prefer not to work behind a desk at a computer again, but I want to do something I'm passionate about and will enhance my life." If I'd have said this to her a year previously, she'd have brushed me off. She used to say, "I'll never get to retire and I'll end up a greeter at Wal-Mart!" I'd reply, "If you keep saying and thinking that, you will."

Now that she was listening to the Abraham Hicks tapes, she was in the right frame of mind to take on this new challenge in her life. When she called me, she'd say she felt for the first time in her life that there was hope for her future.

It took a few weeks for us to get in to see the next referral, Dr. Griswald, a specialist in adult and child neurology. He seemed nice and appeared to be very caring. He turned out to be a good listener, which was a pleasant surprise. He listened to our stories of the experiences we'd had with the 10 doctors we'd already seen and was interested to learn what they thought was going on with Diane. He showed her a picture of a very simple sketch of a box in perspective and asked her to copy it, but she couldn't even get close. She made light of it, as she always did, saying, "I never could draw."

Dr. Griswald had Diane answer some questions and then asked her to remember a few items he'd ask her to repeat in a few minutes. I tried very hard to memorize them, but by the time he asked her to repeat them, I'd forgotten one. Not Diane—she remembered them all!

Dr. Griswald kept everything very light and made us laugh a few times. He had Diane stick out her tongue and when she did he said, "Now you do that to all the rest of those doctors you've seen." Finally, someone with a sense of humor!

He said in a very cheerful way, "I think I know what's going on here, but I need to have a test done to find out for sure." He wanted Diane to have a PET scan (positron emission tomography), which is similar to an MRI, but much more precise. Because it was expensive—several thousand dollars—he said he only requested a few a year from the insurance companies. He said it wouldn't hurt for me to call Diane's primary doctor and request the PET scan, too. He felt the other doctors might have been exaggerating her reaction to their tests, such as the right toe curling up.

As we left Dr. Griswald's office, Diane started telling me I was going to marry him. She thought he was so cute and funny and caring, and he wasn't wearing a wedding ring. She never stopped looking for a husband for me. I was 47 and by choice had never married. She, on the other hand, had been married twice and lived with another man for seven years, which in California equates to marriage; so I teased her about being married three times and said that was enough for both of us. As for this potential husband, I pointed out that he had a hole in the bottom of his shoe. Yes, I have a thing about men's shoes—but that's not germane to this story, which is Diane's.

It took a few weeks, but the insurance company approved the PET scan. I met with Diane at the clinic in Encinitas and sat with her while she waited to go in; she was a little nervous about this one. They said it would take about an hour and a half. Radioactive substance was injected into her bloodstream and she went into the machine for the brain scan. I was told when I picked her up that the report would be instantly available to Dr. Griswald via e-mail.

I took Diane out to lunch and when I got back to my office, I called Dr. Griswald's office and set up a meeting for Monday. This was Friday and I really didn't want to wait any longer than necessary to find out the news. Does she or does she not have dementia?

The Diagnosis

I set up the appointment with Dr. Griswald for late afternoon so I could take Diane out afterward. I told her we were going drinking because we were either going to be celebrating because she didn't have dementia or getting drunk because she did.

We entered the doctor's office with great optimism. Unfortunately, his analysis stunned me so badly I couldn't really remember much else he said after telling us that Diane didn't have dementia, but early-onset Alzheimer's disease!

All I do remember is that I couldn't cry in front of Diane. I had to be strong. I was digging my fingernails into the palm of my hand to hold off the tears, but it just didn't work. The tears came and Diane was, as usual, very stoic. Dr. Griswald asked how she was and she said, "Not very good."

I wished I was as strong as Diane. I knew I needed to get it together so I could ask the right questions, but nothing came out. Dr. Griswald gave Diane a box of a new drug, Namenda, and told her to start taking it right away; it was slowing the progression of Alzheimer's in many patients. Then he said, "Well, if you have to have a disease, at least you got one that doesn't hurt." He was probably trying to make us laugh again, but nothing was going to make me laugh at that point. The entire conversation lasted a short amount of time and when I stood up he said he was sorry.

Alzheimer's disease was first discovered by a German psychiatrist, Alois Alzheimer, in 1906. Almost 100 years of study and still no closer to a cure.—Alz.org

I was still crying as we set up another appointment to see Dr. Griswald in two weeks. We got in the elevator with a woman who was also crying, but her tears were due to acute pain. I told her it was okay—this was the crying elevator—and we chuckled a little.

We walked to the car and Diane already had a positive attitude. She wanted to offer herself to be a "guinea pig" and get involved in finding a cure because she was one of the rare people who were struck with early-onset Alzheimer's. She took one of the Namenda pills as soon as we got in the car.

Instead of going drinking, I felt it was very important we go straight over to Dad's. We found him trimming his avocado trees on the back hill. He was surprised to see us and greeted us with a big smile. As he walked toward us and saw my face, he knew something was wrong. I started crying again and had to go inside. Diane just looked at him and said, "I have Alzheimer's disease." Dad was as shocked as we were and just grabbed Diane and hugged her.

Dorothy, Dad's girlfriend at the time, lived next door, and she called when she saw my car, wondering what was going on. Dad told her the news and she came over right away. Dorothy had just been diagnosed with breast cancer and had to have a mastectomy soon, so this was not an easy time for my dad. He said, "What is happening to all my girls?"

We sat around, had some wine, and discussed everything we'd just learned. We tried to make jokes as we usually did, but this was pretty hard to take lightly. I did jokingly apologize to Dorothy that Diane didn't mean to trump her breast cancer by getting Alzheimer's.

Diane was still the rock among us. She was sure she could beat this. Thank God for the Abraham Hicks tapes! She was equipped with the right attitude, thinking positively, an attitude she was certainly going to need.

After I dropped off Diane, I called our brother, Rick, from my car and told his wife, Trudy, the news. My brother never got on the phone.

Rick is the oldest of the three of us, two years older than Diane. He was always very distant from both Diane and me. He made fun of Diane for being a redhead when she was young and just never wanted much to do with either of us. I was such a tomboy and always wanted to be outside playing "Army man" with Rick and the neighbors, but he never wanted me around.

When we were all teenagers, Rick hardly ever spoke to us. When Diane got married for the first time at 19 and moved out, it left just Rick and me at home. I tried to get to know him, but he wasn't interested. Mom used to always tell me, "I know he acts like he doesn't care about you girls, but he always asks where you are if you aren't home." He always did buy us great Christmas gifts when he got older!

Back in the 1970s, Rick was a really good-looking guy. He was 5'10" with a thin build; had long, thick dark hair and a beard; and dressed pretty cool. My best friend, Trudy, loved to come to our house and try to get his attention because she had such a crush on him—but he ignored her because she was my friend and we were so young. Trudy was very disappointed when he got married.

Rick tied the knot in his mid-20s and I didn't see much of him after that. A few years later, he got a divorce and needed a place to live. I was managing an apartment building my dad owned at the time, and I asked a young couple that was kind of troublesome to leave and told Rick he could move in. He was now my neighbor and we started getting to know each other for the first time in our lives, which was great.

Trudy and I drove to Canada for a vacation one year, and when we returned to San Diego, she stayed the night before leaving for LA, where she lived. I told her Rick was living downstairs and asked if she'd like to say hello. She jumped at the opportunity because she'd never gotten over her crush. To make a long story short, they ended up married and she took him away to LA. I remember the day his moving truck was pulling away; I was in tears because I was just getting to know my brother for the first time and now he was gone again.

Rick and Trudy have been married for 25 years and they now live in Hawaii. I still don't know my brother very well. I love him and know he's a great guy, but we've never had the opportunity to become really close except for some vacations together.

All this aside, I was still wondering why he hadn't called me back after hearing the devastating news about Diane. I needed and would have appreciated a little support!

The Holistic Path

The day after getting the earth-shattering diagnosis, I had to cancel all my appointments because I couldn't stop crying. Actually, there were not too many days after that I didn't cry.

I read about Aricept and Namenda and realized they were both drugs that have only a short-term effect—maybe six months at most—and there was no proven cure for Alzheimer's disease. Perhaps if Diane had been diagnosed correctly the previous year, Aricept could have worked for a while, but because she wasn't, we lost that chance.

If there was nothing that could cure Diane with traditional medicine, I needed to try the alternative, which was holistic medicine. I couldn't just watch her go down this road without a fight!

I called my aunt and uncle, my godparents, Earling and Vonnie Sevik. They had been entirely holistic for years and were very informed about medical issues. Uncle Earl studied reflexology and considered himself to be somewhat of a "hands-on healer." I told them about Diane's diagnosis and what she'd been going through for the past 10 months. They suggested I bring her to Grand Junction, Colorado, to see their healer, Rose. I was ready to put Diane on a plane the next day, but Vonnie said she'd talk to Rose first and call me back.

Vonnie was always my favorite aunt. She was younger than the other aunts and so beautiful inside and out. She was very petite, with dark hair, brown eyes, brown skin, and full lips that enhanced her great smile. I saw her as very quiet and sweet, but very strong, and I tried to be a lot like her in many ways. We both do everything ourselves without asking for help, hate to talk on the phone or buy clothes, love working in the garden, and aren't great in the kitchen. After I lost my mother, she and Earl always watched over me from afar as good godparents do.

The next morning Vonnie called to say that she'd met with Rose and had a list of all the things we needed to do—and she felt Diane would be fine. I was elated and for some reason totally believed her. I had nothing else to believe in.

Vonnie told me to buy the book Brain Recovery by Dr. David Perlmutter, a board-certified neurologist. We needed to do everything he said regarding diet and supplements. We needed to get all her fillings out of her mouth, and then we needed to find someone to do blood chelation. My Uncle Earl had just gone through blood chelation for pain in his legs.

Uncle Earl, my mother's brother, is such a character and he looks like Colonel Sanders of KFC fame. My mom and Earl are both 100% Norwegian, and many years ago several of us traveled together to Norway to a family reunion. While on a boat trip through the fjords, a German couple kept looking at him but they couldn't communicate with him because they didn't speak much English. Finally, the woman started digging through her purse and pulled out a

KFC wipe with Colonel Sanders' picture on it; they wanted to know if he was the Colonel. Our whole group starting laughing hysterically!

After Uncle Earl had bypass surgery, he was put on Coumadin. Even in his mid-70s, he played racquetball several times a week, but suddenly his legs hurt so much he had trouble walking. Vonnie said she'd also noticed that Earl was getting very forgetful and she was a bit concerned that he may be getting Alzheimer's (something she never told him). As I mentioned before, his sister has dementia, so of course Vonnie was worried.

In Vonnie's research, she discovered that Coumadin could have some bad side effects but it could be removed from a person's system through blood chelation; so that's what she had Earl do. After he finished his chelating treatments, she said he had no more pain in his legs, and his brain was functioning much more like the old Earl's.

I asked one of my clients, a doctor, if he'd heard this about Coumadin, and he told me it's one of the most dangerous drugs on the market. The fact that Diane had been on it for a year after her pulmonary embolism now had me a little concerned.

Uncle Earl was not a big fan of doctors and until he had to have his surgery, he thought they were all quacks. After his bypass, he thought perhaps his two surgeons were okay, but he was still leery of other doctors. I guess after listening to him for so many years, I admit I sometimes felt the same way, even though I'd never really had anything wrong with my health and had no negative personal experiences.

I felt I had no alternative but to try the holistic route with Diane.

It was amazing how everything came together after my conversation with Vonnie. I had to run out to one of my job sites and meet with my friend and faux finisher, Denise Cerro, the person who originally loaned me the Abraham Hicks tapes. Denise and all my friends were very much aware of what Diane was going through because it had become so much a part of my life. I was very excited after talking to Vonnie and told Denise everything she said we needed to do. When I mentioned blood chelating, Denise said her friend Dr. Mike Drummen had an alternative clinic in Encinitas. She gave me his home number and I immediately called him. We set up an appointment for a few weeks later and I felt as though we were getting on track.

Diane had told me within a few days of taking the new drug, Namenda, that she was dizzy and had blurred vision in one eye. When she called the doctor, he told her to stop taking the pills for a few days and then start them again.

While waiting for our appointment with Dr. Drummen, I set up a meeting with Lisa Renee Downs, a family member who works with alternative healing methods. I wanted to see what she thought of my plan of attack. We hooked up Diane to the QX machine Lisa used to get our first reading. A little back-story about Lisa and the QX is necessary at this juncture.

Lisa Renee's dad, Jack, is my brother's brother-in-law. I've known him for more than 25 years, and as I mentioned before, he calls himself our plastic brother-in-law. Lisa Renee and I saw each other at family gatherings, such as the one Jack and his wife, Claudia, hosted before Rick and Trudy (Claudia's sister) moved to Hawaii.

Lisa Renee had been into many new and interesting things, and we disappeared into a corner, as we often did when our family got together, to discuss what was going on in her life. She'd told me some time ago she was destined to be a healer and the pull had become so intense that she was being completely drawn into this way of seeing the world. She also told me about a man she'd met who was training her on a QX machine, a laptop that stores people's medical information and works via bio-feedback. Apparently, NASA created it to oversee astronauts' health while they were in space.

Lisa Renee asked me if I wanted to check it out, and I said sure. I'd had a couple of drinks, it was late into the party, and I wasn't quite sure what I was in for. She had me lie down on the bed, and she put straps around my head and each wrist and ankle. The machine then started reading the condition of all the organs in my body; it would send up red flags if it saw any problems.

The first thing it saw was liver damage, which I equated to my drinking that evening. I'm not a big drinker—a glass of wine a few times a week is it—so a couple of drinks in one night was a lot for me. Lisa Renee then became very concerned that my immune system was working at only 40% capacity and my cell regeneration capacity was at 4 out of 10. She saw skin cancer, which I knew I had, and it was attacking my nervous system. I said that was impossible! I eat well, run 15 miles a week, and take very good care of myself. I take a lot of vitamins and consider myself a very healthy person. I pretty much brushed off the whole experience, saying, "Thanks for the exam, that was fun," but I really didn't believe it.

Fast-forward five months. I'd had a few spots of basal cell carcinoma removed from my skin over the years and had given up sun worshiping (a little too late since what we do to our bodies before age 18 comes back and bites us in our 40s). Being half Norwegian and the rest English, Irish, German, etc., and living in sunny San Diego is not a good combination. Throw in the fact I was a real tomboy, am a sports enthusiast, and love to garden, and I really didn't have a chance.

I'd discovered a basal cell carcinoma on my chest and found a plastic surgeon to remove it. While he was taking my stitches out, I asked him to look at a tiny spot on my right nostril. He did a biopsy and said it too was basal cell, but this one was going to involve a little more surgery.

I had to wait a few weeks to get scheduled and in the meantime another one had shown up on my chest. This, too, was cancer.

I had Mohs surgery, named after the doctor who invented it. The surgeon took a small piece off my nose, and I waited while they biopsied it to see if they got it all or had to go back in. By doing this, they don't take any more of the nose (valuable real estate, they called it) than they have to. After four return appointments, several hours, and 30 shots in my nose, most of the perimeter of my nostril had been removed.

Now I had to have reconstructive surgery. The surgeon had to create a flap from the area under my eye and pull the skin down to cover up the area he had just removed. When I got in the elevator to go home, a little boy standing next to me was staring up at me and he looked scared. I then looked at myself in the mirrored walls of the elevator and saw my face. Oh my God! I cried as I drove myself home. What started as a simple little procedure that morning turned into eight hours of horror and I now looked like the "Elephant Man." I ended up having to go through two more plastic surgeries to try to get my nostril back.

A few weeks after this, our family met for the October birthdays. Jack, Lisa Renee, Dad, and I all had birthdays within a few of weeks of each other, and we tried to meet for dinner to celebrate them together. When Lisa Renee saw me with my face still bandaged she asked, "Now will you let me work with you?" It really hit me; this is what she had tried to warn me about when she hooked me up to the QX machine five months earlier!

At Rick and Trudy's going away party, Lisa Renee had said she saw skin cancer attacking my nervous system and my immune system was very low. After that, my interior design business had been extremely busy, which equates to me having an extreme level of stress—not to mention what I'd been going through with Diane. Stress depletes the immune system. No matter how well you think you're doing or feeling, you never really know until something like this happens. Skin cancer is my weakness, so that's how it affected me. Someone else may have a heart attack.

I began working with Lisa Renee right away. She'd hook me up to the QX machine to get a reading of what my body was doing and then it would go into its cell regeneration mode. Lisa Renee brought in her own healers from "the other side" to work on me while I was hooked up to the machine. She was actually channeling this medical team. I know it sounds strange, but I wouldn't have believed it if I hadn't experienced it myself. I was getting the benefits of medical technology and old-fashioned healing at the same time.

I'd known Lisa Renee for 20 years and she was just a normal person up until the last few years. She had no medical background at all, so for me to lie there and hear what was coming out of her mouth was amazing.

Lisa Renee had me start on several supplements and do many cleanses. She hooked me up with a biochemist, Mitch, who'd created a product for cancer victims that helps create glutathione, which is needed to build up the disease-depleted immune system. Within four months, the QX machine was telling me that my immune system was working at 95% capacity and my cell regeneration capacity was 10 out of 10.

Diane was very curious about what I was going through and was totally intrigued with what Lisa Renee was doing for me. She decided to see if Lisa Renee could help her with her tinnitus, ringing in her ears she'd had for years that drove her crazy. She went to Lisa Renee once, but was disappointed her condition wasn't cured after that visit and never went back.

Dad also listened to my stories and decided he would see if Lisa Renee could help him with his enlarged prostate. After one visit, he told me he'd slept through the night without having to get up and use the bathroom for the first time in years! He, too, only went one time, and his problem came back. It takes several treatments to solve health issues and neither Diane nor my dad wanted to invest the necessary time and effort.

At my next meeting with Lisa Renee, she told me Diane had some brain damage show up when she was working on her for the tinnitus. She'd asked her if she'd ever had a blow to the head or a head injury. Lisa Renee said there was a lot going on in Diane's head and more than one session would be needed to resolve the problems. There were some really serious blockage issues.

Back to Diane's session with Lisa Renee. I'd read the book Vonnie recommended about brain recovery and had already started to put some of the things in it into action. Lisa Renee agreed with everything the book said and added much more to the routine. She knew about Mike Drummen's clinic; in fact, Jack and Claudia had gone to him for treatments. This was confirmation we were going in the right direction.

As we were leaving, I asked Lisa Renee to muscle-test Diane for Namenda, which Dr. Griswald wanted her to get back on; I was afraid of it after her dizzy spell and blurred vision. During muscle testing, a person holds whatever is being testing for in one hand and holds the other arm straight out and rigid while the practitioner pushes down on it. If the body tests negatively for the object, in this case Namenda, the arm will just go limp. If it tests positively, the arm will stay rigid. Diane muscle-tested very negatively toward Namenda, which confirmed to me we should keep her off it for now.

Lisa Renee felt we really needed to clean all the toxins from Diane's body, and adding another drug would only complicate things. She said she couldn't make the decision for us, but Diane and I discussed it and we both felt it was not necessary to continue the Namenda.

To confirm my feelings, I called Cindy, one of my design clients who works as a sales rep for Namenda, told her about Diane, and asked her opinion. She said they'd had great results with the drug on older Alzheimer's patients, including her grandmother, but she didn't know of anyone using it at such a young age. I told her I really felt we needed to go the holistic route for right now.

Because Diane was so young, I truly felt we could rid her of this terrible disease. Cindy noted that Namenda only slows the condition and doesn't cure it, and those who stop taking it may get worse. That was all I needed to hear to convince me that Diane didn't need this drug right now. I was thankful she'd been on it for only a few days before they took her off because of the dizzy spells and blurred vision.

I called my dad at that point and told him I really didn't want Diane to go back on Namenda. I told him about the group of healers that had surrounded us. I wanted him to give me six months to work on healing Diane holistically and most importantly, fund it, because insurance didn't cover any of it except for a percentage of the dental work. He agreed because he knew I was doing what I thought was best for Diane, and he trusted me.

Dad came to me several times over the next few months to ask me if I was certain we were doing the right thing. I said I didn't know for sure, but I really felt we had no alternative. The only drug out there wasn't a cure and could cause more harm than good in the long run. I wasn't interested in just slowing it down; I was interested in stopping it! He still questioned me from time to time, but I just kept reminding him of his promise to give me six months.

In the meantime, Dad had to take over all of Diane's personal finances, very much against her will. She was adamant about even showing Dad her checkbook, but when we finally convinced her we just wanted to help, we discovered it was a little too late. She'd not been taking care of her finances for some time and was pretty deep in the hole. We really should have done something long ago, but we just assumed she was still able to do it herself. Talk about being in total denial! We were very wrong; her downward financial spiral had apparently been going on for a few years. She'd gotten into money trouble and had refinanced her condo twice, taking out extra cash to help pay off her bills. The mortgage on her condo, which Dad had helped her buy, should have been substantially paid down, but it was actually higher than when they bought it!

Dad took over her checkbook and was responsible for paying all her bills and maintaining her car. I was responsible for all the medical and insurance work. We didn't want Diane to worry about anything except getting well; we'd take care of the rest.

It seems Diane had lost the ability to add or subtract some time ago. She joked about it, saying she'd always hated math, but one night when we were out to dinner and the bill came, I had to help her figure out the tip. I told her she should leave $3 for the $17 ticket. She just sat there and looked at me, waiting for me to tell her the sum of 3 and 17. Around this time I read an article in which a man described what it felt like to be in the early stages of Alzheimer's. He called the tangles in his brain "gunk in his noggin." When I told Diane this, she laughed, so whenever we talked about her confusion or she couldn't pull up a word she was searching for, I'd say, "It's okay, you have gunk in your noggin," and it would always make her laugh.

Tangles destroy a vital cell transport system made of proteins. This system is organized in orderly parallel strands somewhat like railroad tracks. Food molecules, cell parts and other key materials travel along the "tracks." A protein called tau (rhymes with wow) helps the tracks stay straight. In areas where tangles are forming, Tau collapse into twisted strands called tangles. The tracks can no longer stay straight. They fall apart and disintegrate.—Alz.org

Diane had previously been a great speller. I know because I am the world's worst, and I'd called her at work many times when I just couldn't figure out how to spell a word, usually after using my Franklin Speller, then going to the computer and then the dictionary. What I've found about spelling is that if you don't know how a word starts, you can't even look it up! I remember when a client wanted me to create a space in her home for her to practice her cello; for the life of me I couldn't figure out how to spell cello because I assumed it started with "ch". Doesn't it sound like cello would start with a "ch"? I didn't realize at the time it was an Italian word.

Diane would usually be very patient and not laugh too hard at me. Once we hung up, I'm sure she shared these phone calls with the people in the office and they all had a good laugh. My favorite saying was by Thomas Jefferson: "Tis a might poor man indeed that can think of only one way to spell a word."

Diane finally bought me the book Spelling for Dummies, which allows you to look up a word the way you think it should be spelled and usually, there it is! For instance, if I were trying to spell guinea pig, I'd look up "ginny pig" to get the correct spelling. I think of Diane every time I use my "dummy speller," which is often!

I know we're all brought into this world, for the most part, with a perfectly good running body. We tend to screw it up by how we take care of it, but I'm also convinced we can repair it and get it functioning properly again if we believe we can and want it badly enough.

Diane was started on a host of supplements, and according to the book Brain Recovery, we now needed to clean out her kitchen and get rid of salt and pepper shakers with metal tops, aluminum foil, and aluminum cookie sheets and pans of any kind. Everything in the kitchen that contained aluminum—including all canned foods—had to go. Next was the bathroom. It's amazing how many things that contain aluminum, such as deodorant and lotion, we put on our skin daily and that aluminum is ingested into our bodies. We made lists of everything we needed to buy holistic to replace every aluminum-containing thing in Diane's house.

Being such a great soul, Diane took it all on as an exciting challenge. She'd always been a list maker and loved to organize things, so this was right up her alley.

From all the books I'd read, I came to the conclusion that Diane's diet was going to be almost vegan. She never complained about that, either. She was so determined we were going to beat this disease that she'd do anything we told her to do with a smile on her face.

The day came when we finally got to meet Dr. Drummen at the alternative clinic. He was in his mid-40s, nice looking, and very quiet and soft-spoken. He didn't say much at the first meeting. When I mentioned this to Diane, she said he was probably bowled over by me because I rattled off everything we'd gone through for the past 11 months and all the steps we'd taken since the diagnosis a few weeks ago—all within five minutes of meeting him. She said he probably just didn't know how to react to me. I guess I was just a little excited.

Dr. Drummen admitted he'd never treated an Alzheimer's patient, but he thought he could help. I asked him if he was familiar with the QX machine Lisa Renee was using and he said he was, but he'd be working on Diane using a biomeridian machine, which he felt was a much more practical and usable tool. He said they both had pros and cons, but the biomeridian machine worked in ways we could understand a little better and he could make specific changes. He could check the alpha lipoic acid, which is an important nutrient in protecting the brain, and find out how much Diane required.

He wanted to determine exactly how much of some of the most important vitamins and supplements Diane's body required and get an idea of what was causing the clouding in her brain. He said the tendency to have sluggish blood is caused by toxins in general, but we needed to discover what specific toxins were the culprits in Diane. We wanted concrete answers about whether they were heavy metal toxins or non-heavy-metal toxins.

Dr. Drummen wanted to start Diane on blood chelation as soon as possible. We were on board with that given our Uncle Earl's positive experience. In chelation, via an IV, a product would be put in Diane's blood to attract and gather the metals, which would then be eliminated through her urine or bowel movements. This would require that she be hooked up to an IV for three hours twice a week for 20 or 30 sessions. Phew!

Dr. Drummen said all we were hoping for was that two to five years into the future, Diane would be at the same place she was now, no worse. Because these natural therapies are highly variable, there was no way to predict how Diane would respond and how well it would work until we tried.

Before starting chelation, Diane needed to start taking an enzyme that cleared up circulation. The enzyme would "chew up" debris in the blood during detox. Fabrazyme was the one she was prescribed.

We were told it wouldn't do any good to start the blood chelation until Diane had her fillings removed, and we were referred to a holistic dentist. I asked what made a dentist holistic and learned they use special equipment for removing fillings that protects both the patient and the dentist from the mercury. An electromagnetic field pulls all the mercury vapors out of the way and then a suction device pulls the exhaust away. Patients get oxygen that flows through their nose so they have natural, clean air to breathe. Finally, instead of drilling out fillings, the dentist uses a tool to cut them into small chunks so there isn't as much dust.

Dr. Drummen told us as soon as we set up the dental appointment that Diane needed to return to his clinic to get a Vitamin C IV drip to build up her immune system for the procedure. Diane had seven fillings that needed to be extracted, so this took a few weeks.

Diane had some wonderful neighbors, Ken and Gene, an older couple with whom she'd become good friends. Diane would occasionally ask Ken for assistance with something and she'd always buy him nonalcoholic beer as payment. They always watched over Diane's place when she was out of town and were generally the perfect next-door neighbors. Ken loved to bake and after I told him my favorite birthday cake was a white cake with white frosting and coconut, he made me one! He was so sweet.

I asked Diane if she'd told Ken and Gene that she had Alzheimer's and she said no. She didn't want them to know. She didn't want them to worry about her burning the house down or doing something else that would affect them. (They shared a connecting wall.) I thought this was kind of a strange thing for her to say, but maybe this was a fear she had.

Diane said she didn't want anyone to know because she didn't want to be treated differently. I tried to explain to her it was nothing to be embarrassed about, and it was probably better if she told people what was going on so they'd understand why she was having trouble communicating. Most people probably knew something was wrong because she'd been off work for close to a year.

Dr. Drummen next set up a meeting with his colleague, Dr. Jeffers, who had a Ph.D. in nutrition, to have Diane tested on the biomeridian machine. After we got the results from this test, along with urine tests, these doctors were better able to see exactly what her body was doing and what it needed. They removed many more foods from Diane's diet because they felt she was allergic to them. She had Candida, so all wheat was removed. She showed allergies to beans (there went her favorite Mexican food), all dairy (there went ice cream, her other favorite food), and eventually soy products. Because she could have no sugar, that meant no fruit or fruit juices (or chocolate, which she insisted on every day). She could have two poached eggs a week and a little chicken and beef but no seafood, which was no problem for Diane because she hated fish. She could eat most vegetables except carrots and tomatoes because of the sugar content. Finding things she could eat became more and more of a challenge.

I took Diane shopping at Jimbo's, a well-known San Diego natural grocer, to search for new things she could eat and get some help from the employees. We discovered cereals made from rice that were not too bad, goat cheese prepared many different ways, RICE DREAM products to substitute for milk, and some different types of soy products with which to experiment. Diane was told to pour lots of olive oil on everything she ate. She went home with great enthusiasm to try her discoveries in some new recipes.

Lisa Renee also recommended that Diane have weekly full body massages to increase her blood circulation, which was one of the problems the QX had shown. She had only a 65% flow of blood to her brain. It had become apparent to us that she had bad circulation and that's what probably caused her to have the pulmonary embolism. We sent her to a great guy I'd gone to in Carlsbad, Darin. He took great interest in Diane's whole recovery program and was very patient when she got confused and went to the wrong office (she went to the alternative clinic) for their first massage appointment.

Because Diane became confused so easily, I made a calendar every month showing all her appointments. She hadn't missed one since that first day. On the days when she wasn't hooked up to the IV, getting a massage, or having a session with Lisa Renee, I wrote down "power walk." I said her "job" was to keep her circulation flowing by exercising as often as she could. She loved to drive to Mission Beach and do her power walks of four miles or so along the boardwalk. Some weeks, she had every day packed with healing sessions.

At Diane's July 1, 2005, session with Lisa Renee, we learned the blood circulation to her brain was at 95%, a far cry from the 65% it was just three months earlier. It looked as though things were working!

I began to be concerned that Diane was getting too thin. She'd lost a lot of weight since everything started over a year earlier. She'd gone from a size 12 to a size 6, which isn't necessarily a bad thing, but she was looking quite frail and I asked Dr. Drummen if he could help us with her diet.

Dr. Drummen asked Diane to bring all the supplements she'd been taking to her next appointment so he could test and organize them for her and modify her existing nutritional panel. He then gave her a little kit and told her she needed to check her pH level on a regular basis and keep it between 6 and 6.5. She also needed to add hydrochloric acid and pancreatic acid for digestion. He finished the session by saying it could take 40 to 60 sessions of blood chelating to see improvement. Damn!

I'd asked Dr. Drummen what Dr. Jeffers was doing with Diane, because she'd told me she had to sleep on the sofa to avoid being around chicken feathers! Because she got things mixed up a lot, I kind of chuckled and thought she'd misunderstood something. When I asked her about it, she didn't know why her pillow and down comforter were off limits for 24 hours. Dr. Drummen gave me a book to read about clearings and told me I should go with Diane to the next meeting she had with Dr. Jeffers to check it out.

I was amazed when I began reading the book that night. Say Good-Bye to Illness was written by Devi S. Nambudripad, M.D., D.C., L.Ac., Ph.D. (Acu.), an Indian woman born with allergies to almost everything in her world. She could wear only silk because any other material would make her severely ill. She lived on white rice and broccoli for over a year because her system couldn't tolerate anything else. She discovered something she named Nambudripad's Allergy Elimination Technique (NAET), which has been taught for years to hundreds of doctors and practitioners all over the world to cure people of their allergies.

I was able to see this technique in action when I went with Diane to see Dr. Jeffers. He was in his mid-40s, tall, thin, and redheaded, a good-looking Swede from Jamestown, North Dakota, where everyone in my family (except me) was born. He was very nice and answered all my many questions. We discussed the NAET he was using on Diane and he showed me how it worked. He'd studied under Dr. Nambudripad for 20 years and had even written an article in her book.

Dr. Jeffers laid Diane on her back, put vials of different things in her hand, and muscle-tested her for them. At this session, he put a vial of avocado in her left hand and had her hold it on her tummy while she held her right arm up rigid so he could apply pressure to it to see how it reacted. Luckily, her arm held rigid so he let her continue to eat avocadoes.

Dr. Jeffers told me about Dr. Nambudripad's latest test. She'd been able to get autistic children with no verbal skills to speak by using the technique for several sessions. It had also been used to cure children who suffer from peanut allergies so they could live more normal lives.

Dr. Jeffers laid Diane on her stomach and used this strange device to quickly trigger the meridians down her back. He then put her in the waiting room to massage certain parts of her body for several minutes. She massaged her elbow for a few seconds, which stimulated her small intestine; then her hand, which stimulated her large intestine; then four fingers up from her ankle on her leg, which stimulated her spleen; and then the top of her foot, which stimulated her liver. She massaged each for a few seconds over and over again while holding a vial of something in her hand that I later found out was calcium. That's what her body told him he needed to clear that day, so she needed to be off calcium for 24 hours. This situation was similar to the one with the feathers, which I learned were eliminated to clear a chicken allergy that came up during the previous session.

I was finding this all so fascinating! I was thrown into a world I'd never have experienced otherwise. I was so hoping I'd be able to share some of this information to help others. The next week a client told me her granddaughter had just been diagnosed with peanut allergies and she was so worried about how the restrictions would affect her life. I was excited to tell her about NAET and how it was able to cure these types of allergies, but she looked at me like I was crazy. I don't know if she ever shared it with her daughter or they ever checked it out. What I have found out about all of this is that while I've always had an open mind to alternative medicine, many others do not, and you have to be careful who you share these things with, kind of like religion and politics.

Diane went for a clearing with Dr. Jeffers once a week from January to June, approximately 24 sessions, to complete the entire list of clearings recommended by Dr. Nambudripad. Diane drove to the clinic once a week, but I went to each session with her so I could communicate with the doctor because Diane's conversations had become very simple and basic. Dad sat in on one session to watch how it was done, but had a difficult time believing in all of it. He questioned me constantly about what we were doing, but finally realized he just needed to trust us.

I also had to be there so I could sit with her and help her massage the four pressure points after each session. No matter how hard she tried, she couldn't remember the four points on her body and keep track of what point she'd just done. She'd get really embarrassed when we sat in the waiting room with everyone watching as I pointed to the area on her body to go to next, but she learned to deal with it. She was cleared of all allergies, her body was in complete balance, and she could now eat anything she wanted.

Along with these clearings, Diane was also driving to Carlsbad to get massages from Darin, her massage therapist. Massage is very important when you're going through this type of clearing so your circulation keeps moving and eliminating toxins from the body. Darin took a personal interest in Diane and would call me often to see how she was doing. He bought her a brainteaser game to help stimulate her senses. Diane and I played it once, but it was too much for her. She was quite fond of Darin, but when she lost her driver's license (that story is to come), the massage therapy was one of the things she had to give up.

Diane was also having colonics done every six weeks or so, something that helps remove toxins more quickly. This was not one of her favorite things to go through, but Diane seldom complained. She was such an angel in that way; she just took everything in stride no matter what new process I arranged for her.

Dimebon, a drug that has been in phase three of clinical trials for treatment of Alzheimer's disease, has recently been discontinued after studies concluded it was ineffective.—About.com

As I mentioned above, Diane eventually lost her driving privileges. It began as an error by the DMV, but was probably a blessing in disguise. Dad received a letter from Diane's car insurance company telling her it was going to cancel her insurance because she'd been driving on an expired license for four months. He marched down to the DMV to find out what had happened. The day Dr. Griswald diagnosed Diane with Alzheimer's, he told us that by law he had to notify the DMV of her condition and she'd be called in to take written and driving tests. In response, they sent Diane a letter asking her to come in and be tested, but it was sent to an old address and she never received it.

Once Diane learned she'd have to be tested, she went right down to the DMV and got a handbook so she could start studying. We knew her short-term memory was pretty bad, but her long-term comprehension was still great. Because she'd been driving since she was 16, we hoped her long-term memory would kick in and she'd ace the test! That was my thinking, anyway. She said she wasn't worried about the driving part of it.

Diane studied for weeks for the written DMV exam. Both Dad and I spent many hours reviewing sample tests with her trying to help her get ready. I was worried when I would read the questions to her and she'd get them wrong. When I tried to explain to her that she just needed to think about it, I could see she was no longer able to rationalize simple scenarios dealing with road laws. She insisted the tests must be wrong because they didn't make sense.

One day when I was driving with Diane, she entered a busy intersection on a yellow light to turn left. When the light turned red, I said she could go, but she just sat there in a panic. One other time she pulled right in front of a car coming at us. In retrospect, I let her drive far too long. I realize now that deep in my heart I was afraid of her losing her license, which meant she was losing her independence, and maybe proved that what we were doing wasn't working.

Dad took Diane for the written test and she was given an extra long time. However, she couldn't complete it in the time allotted and she failed. Her vision was so bad that she was having trouble reading, and we helped her get new reading glasses so she could try it again. She studied her heart out again, but failed a second time.

The Traditional Path

On October 10, 2005, my plastic brother-in-law, Jack, turned 60. He rented a wonderful house in Arrowhead and invited the whole gang, 17 of us, for a three-day weekend to help him celebrate. Rick and Trudy, who hadn't seen Diane for some time, came over from Hawaii for the big event.

At one point everyone was playing pool and tried to get Diane to join in. Our friend Mike said he wanted her on his team. We all stood around stunned when Diane forgot how to hold the pool cue. We were brought up with a pool table in our garage, so Diane was very familiar with the game. Mike was a doll. He put his arms around her and guided her with the cue, showing her how to hit the white ball first and aim it toward the ball she was trying to get in the pocket. Every time it was her turn, this same procedure had to be done; Diane couldn't remember how to hold and aim the cue. She was extremely quiet the whole weekend, too. There was just too much stimulation and chatter for her to keep up.

Diane had always been such a chatterbox. She'd drive me crazy because it seemed she never stopped talking! I took her on a two-week driving trip to New England once and I had to learn how to tune her out because she chattered away the whole time. Seeing how quiet she'd become, I had a great deal of guilt, remembering how I'd wished she would just shut up. As they say, be careful what you wish for.

Rick and Trudy had moved to Hawaii before Diane's mental health declined, so they hadn't been around to see it. They were shocked at her behavior and began questioning me about the holistic route I'd had taken with her. Dad had said he didn't mind if I tried an alternative path for six months and then reassessed the situation. After seeing her now, Dad, Rick, and Trudy felt we also needed to try traditional medicine.

I was irritated that I'd been doing everything I could to help Diane and suddenly they were telling me Diane should go to a "regular" doctor, even knowing the traditional doctor can't do a thing! Rick and Trudy hadn't been around to help in any way, but they felt they knew what we should do! I was very frustrated.

A few days before our Arrowhead gathering, I'd returned home and probably was a little jet lagged after a wonderful two-week vacation traveling through northern Italy and Tuscany, which brings us back to the beginning of this story.

I'd felt for a long time, and still do, that Tuscany is where I want to live one day. I loved logging onto "International Living" and looking at real estate in Tuscany. I found several little fixer-uppers that were very reasonably priced. I'd get so excited that I could hardly wait to become an expat.

My travels had taken me to some wonderful places around the world, but I'd been saving Tuscany for my honeymoon. By this time I was heading for my 50th birthday and had never been married, but this was still a special dream of mine. I was starting to feel a little more open to marriage at this point in my life, possibly because I was approaching the big 5-0 and I didn't want to travel alone when I retired. It had become very obvious to me that my travel buddy, Diane, who was always my backup travel companion, would no longer be there for me.

Whenever Diane and I would see a couple of little old ladies together arm and arm chatting away, we'd always say, "That'll be us when we're 80!" It brings me to tears now whenever I see a pair of little old ladies, knowing that wasn't our destiny.

As it turns out, I ended up going to Tuscany before a honeymoon was even a possibility because a very good friend of mine, Darleen, had planned a trip to go there with her husband, Doug, but he unexpectedly died of a misdiagnosed pulmonary embolism (ironically, the same fate that could have befallen Diane). The day she told me about his death, she asked me to take her to Italy. She said Doug would have wanted her to still go on the trip, and I was the only experienced traveler she knew who'd take her—so of course I said yes. However, the long train rides looking at the Tuscan countryside were very painful at times, knowing unless I could find a cure for Diane, my dream of living here couldn't come true.

It was a wonderful journey, but I admit I was a little disappointed to be enjoying my dream destination with a girlfriend. When I shared this feeling with a friend before we left, she suggested, "Maybe this is a good thing. Perhaps you're destined to go on this trip now and you'll find your husband in Tuscany!"

As usual, Diane stayed at my house while I was in Italy and took care of my two cats. One day, she laid out all her vitamins on the kitchen counter to take the following day. Unfortunately, my most adventurous cat, Cinder, couldn't resist Diane's fish oil capsule. She took it, dropped it on the carpet, and bit into it, staining the carpet with brown oil. When Diane saw it the next morning, she hurried to the store to buy some carpet cleaner, but instead of spaying a little bit on the spot, she poured the entire bottle on the stain.

When I got home there was a two-foot-diameter stain on my new carpet. I had a Hoover carpet-cleaning machine and after several hours I was able to suck up all the soap. Poor Diane, she was getting so confused.

I'd made Diane a promise when she was first diagnosed with Alzheimer's that I would take her to New York, someplace she'd always dreamed of going. I'd already been twice, but loved the city so it was definitely no problem for me. I was, however, planning a trip to Washington, D.C., with Joshua, a long-time friend. We'd been traveling together for the past few years, trying to visit one major city each year.

Joshua is one of my dearest friends. We met when I was managing my dad's apartment building in the mid-1970s. He moved in downstairs from me when he relocated to San Diego from Seattle to take a job with McDonnell Douglas, where he worked on the designs of their airplanes.

Joshua is an attractive Swede with a great wit and is very intelligent. We'd sit around our little shared patio with cocktails in hand and talk about our dreams. He really wanted out of aerospace and dreamed of being a journalist like his great uncle, Edward R. Murrow. I wanted out of civil engineering. I was a civil engineering technician for the water district at that time and wanted to be an interior designer. We always supported and encouraged each other, and eventually we both followed our dreams and got our degrees in our chosen professions.

Joshua became a journalist in a small town in the Midwest, and even though we sometimes went long periods of time without speaking, we always kept in touch. He ended up going back into aerospace design and worked out of Long Beach, so we were able to see each other more often.

Joshua and I had visited New York two years ago. I knew Joshua loved the Big Apple as much as I did, so I asked him if he'd be willing to go with us on this trip and put Washington, D.C., off until the following year. He was all for it, proving to be a great friend indeed. A few days after we returned home from Arrowhead, the three of us boarded a plane for New York City. I had to go over to Diane's the night before we left and help her pack to make sure she had the right clothes. Good thing I did, because she had all summer clothes packed and it was October; it would be cold and rainy in New York.

I booked this trip first class because Diane had never experienced anything but coach, and she was really thrilled. We had a great time, but Diane was always so confused that it really scared me. Joshua helped keep an eye on her, but I cried myself to sleep every night because I was so worried about how fast she was declining. She could hardly complete a sentence, couldn't put on her seatbelt in the plane, and couldn't remember how to get from the hotel lobby to our room without my assistance. We almost lost her in the subway one day because she just started walking away. That was pretty scary!

The only place Diane really wanted to go while we were in New York was Serendipity. I guess she had seen a movie, one that I had never seen, in which Serendipity is described as having the best ice cream sundaes anywhere.

Unfortunately, however, we arrived there right after we had eaten lunch and the place turned out to be a restaurant, not an ice cream parlor as we thought. The line was out the door and the wait was very long so we went elsewhere for ice cream. I felt bad for Diane, but as usual she just went with the flow. I think despite the Serendipity disappointment, she had a really great time in New York.

Once we got home, Diane was a completely different person. She was much less confused, she was talking again, and she seemed much more like her old self. I learned she did much better without too much stimulation. She'd spent two weeks at my house cat sitting, went to the Arrowhead house with a large group of noisy people, and then went right off to New York, which in itself is very exciting. She was so overstimulated that she could barely function.

My personal doctor had referred us to a world-renowned neurologist and Alzheimer's specialist who heads up the UCSD Alzheimer's Center. For the first appointment, Dad, Diane, and I went together. I wanted Dad to be part of this, because it was partially his idea. Dr. Thomas was probably in his 70s, about 6'2", and quite lean. I had the most trouble communicating with him of any of the doctors I'd met, most likely because of my frustration after two years of seeing doctors and also because of his brusque manner.

When he allowed me a minute to talk, I told him about all the holistic things we'd been doing for the past six months. He got a very disapproving look on his face and said, "Either you do holistic, which has never been proven to work, or you do traditional medicine!"

Four months later, right before our second meeting with Dr. Thomas, Diane failed her driver's test for the second time. We really didn't see any difference in her after she started taking Aricept. When we told the doctor that Diane had just failed her driver's license test, he said she'd never drive again. He said there was nothing wrong with her vision, but her brain was causing her vision to be blurred and it wouldn't allow her to pass the written test, let alone the driving test. Dad and I sat there in shock at this news. He wanted to put her on a different drug and wrote a prescription for Razadyne.

Dr. Thomas also made me an offer: He said if I was interested, I could have genetic screening done to see if I also had a chance of getting Alzheimer's. I told him, thank you, but I'd prefer not to know.

Diane didn't seem upset at all at the prospect of never driving again. She said, "That's fine. I don't want to study for the test again anyway. It was too difficult. I just want to go get drunk!" It was interesting that when Diane was mad or upset, she seemed to find her words much more easily.

We took Diane to a Mexican restaurant, where she quickly downed two margaritas and we talked more about what we'd just learned. The thought of never being able to drive again would have been a hard pill for me to swallow, but Diane had us laughing about it. She'd never lost her sense of humor through all this, thank God!

Around this time Diane's friend Pam called me to ask if there was anything she could do to help now that Diane couldn't drive. I said she could just be there for her and be her friend; that was what she needed most right then. It would also be great if she could pick up Diane once in a while and take her out for some fun. From that point on, Pam took Diane out to play on Friday nights, just like the "good old days."

I noticed most of Diane's friends didn't call her much anymore. I think they were afraid of the disease and weren't sure how to treat her. It was Diane in there; she was a little less chatty and became confused easily, but she still wanted to enjoy life.

Pam also told me a story that broke my heart. When Diane was still able to drive, she went out to shop for a birthday present for me and called Pam from a shopping center to ask where her two favorite stores, William Sonoma and Victoria's Secret, were located. When Pam asked her what shopping center she was at, she didn't know. Hearing this story made me realize it was a blessing when she lost her license. If she was that disoriented, she shouldn't have been behind the wheel of a car.

What I later learned was Diane became very good at covering up things. If she'd told me that story about being lost in the shopping center, I'd have taken action much sooner. She wanted to keep her independence and was struggling to keep up the façade that she was still able to function quite well on her own.

I still miss our movie nights. Every Friday, I'd pick up Diane after work and we'd see a movie that had just come out. Afterward, we'd go out to dinner and discuss it. She eventually got to the point where she could no longer remember what had happened when the movie was over. One night, we were about a half hour into a dark comedy when she grabbed my arm and said she was sick. I rushed her into the bathroom but she was fine; she just wanted to leave. I think she was upset with the movie and wanted to get out of the theater. We quit going when she was no longer able to understand what the movies were about.

In January 2006, we were off to Hawaii for Trudy's 50th birthday. Dad, Diane, and I went to Kona, where we were surrounded by the gang of 17 again. I remember one day in particular. I'll never forget the look on Trudy's face when we all went snorkeling and she was going to be in charge of Diane because she and Rick snorkeled all the time. Diane had forgotten how to swim, let alone snorkel.

She couldn't even figure out how to put on her mask. She was like a child trying to dog paddle to stay above the water and had a look of panic on her face. We didn't get her a life vest because she'd never liked to wear one. Rick took one arm, Trudy took the other, and they began swimming with her.

A couple in the water was watching this all happen. The lady swam over and gave Trudy and Rick the long foam floating tube she was using while snorkeling. She said, "Here, use this. You can give it back to me when you're done." What a great act of kindness.

One day we all helped Trudy set up her new store, Trudy's Island Art, where she sold local artists' artwork and jewelry. Trudy told Diane to pick a piece of jewelry from her collection as a thank you for helping her. Diane picked out a beautiful pair of earrings. Later in the hotel room, Diane asked if they were mine; she didn't remember Trudy giving them to her.

Diane had never shown much emotion throughout this whole ordeal. I, on the other hand, cried all the time! Her lack of emotion worried me, but when I thought about it, I'd never seen my sister show much emotion at all. A few months earlier, Diane called to tell me that her friend Lavina had died. She was in her mid-70s and a little spitfire of a lady, a Cherokee Indian who was tough as nails. Diane absolutely loved her, and she was crying as she told me about her death. I realized that was the first time I'd heard her cry probably since our mom died.

By now Diane had gone through over 30 chelations. She was really getting burned out on sitting there with a needle in her arm two days a week for three hours, and I certainly didn't blame her. It had also become more difficult now because Dad had to drive her to all her appointments. We decided to find an alternative. Dr. Jeffers told us about magnetic clay, which you put into the bathtub to create a detox bath twice a week; it draws the metal out of your body like chelation but at a slower rate. Diane preferred this method. She took the baths for months and said she really enjoyed them. She had another urine test to check if the baths were working, and her metal levels did seem to be gradually going down.

Diane looked and felt much better. She had such a great figure and was now wearing my clothes. Removing most of the bad carbohydrates and sugar from her diet and adding a lot more greens made the weight just fall off. Up until she'd lost her license, she'd also been driving to the beach two or three times a week to do four-mile power walks; she was in the best shape she'd been in 30 years. Dad now had to pick her up and take her on her walks, which was good for him, too, but they didn't happen as often.

Diane was trying to adjust to losing her license, but it represented a real loss of freedom. Dad now had to take her everywhere. I always spent Sundays with her, taking her to the grocery store, doing other errands, and trying to think of fun things to do. We'd go to local art or street fairs or concerts in the park and then have a nice dinner. Because I lived farther from Diane than Dad did, plus I run my own company, it was harder for me to get there on weekday evenings.

During my search for a holistic cure for Diane, I'd read countless books, Healing Remedies, Brain Recovery, and Mind Boosting Secrets, to name just a few. They were all very informative and we tried everything we thought could possibly work. One day Dr. Jeffers told Diane to bring in her Brita water filter for testing. The results showed it didn't take out the metals he wanted removed, and he asked me to order her a Code Blue water filter. I did so and started talking to the representative about Diane. When he learned she had Alzheimer's, he was very insistent that she start drinking mangosteen juice.

Mangosteen is a fruit that is grown primarily in Africa and China and has been used for medicinal purposes for thousands of years. Its rind has at least 40 super antioxidant xanthones, which contain elements that supposedly help correct imbalances and kill many diseases. It's been tested for years and many medical doctors now promote it. They're seeing remarkable recovery stories involving many different cancers, Parkinson's disease, arthritis, fibromyalgia, etc., but nothing about curing Alzheimer's. That didn't deter me; I'd been saying for a long time that I would try anything!

The company that makes the juice is called Xango, a catchy name that combines mangosteen and xanthones. When I asked Dr. Jeffers about it, he said he was just about ready to tell us about it. He was convinced it would be a good product for Diane to try; in fact, it was soon going to be sold at the clinic. I placed an order right away. I became a distributor to bring the price down to $31 a bottle (about the size of a wine bottle) from $40 retail. After drinking six bottles a month for a few months, Diane seemed to think it was making a difference. In particular, she thought she was able to write a little better than she use to. That was huge!

I also decided to drink the mangosteen juice to build my immune system, and I got Dad to take it for high blood pressure, high cholesterol, and overall good health. He fought me on it all the way, but said he would drink it.

Diane had always had such beautiful penmanship, unlike mine, which is sometimes illegible even to me. However, she was having trouble writing and asked me if I could help her make address labels she could print out on her computer so she could still send cards to all her friends. Diane was the biggest card sender I'd ever met; I'd get a few every month from her for no reason at all. It was so fun to go to the mailbox and get one of her unexpected cards. She always found the best, funniest cards and then she'd write even funnier things in them. I always told her she should have her own card company and then she could hire Rick to write all the sick and demented cards, which was his expertise. I tried for a while to show her how to create labels and even wrote down the process step by step, but as I was going over it, I knew this, too, was way above her ability.

It's always interesting the way things come into our lives. One night I was having dinner with a good friend of mine, Jackie, who's a healer, and I told her about the NAET clearing Diane had been doing. We were just about ready to leave the restaurant when the lady sitting next to me grabbed my arm, apologized for eavesdropping, and said she had to talk to me. She was very familiar with Dr. Jeffers and NAET, but suggested we investigate using another technique, NET (Neuro Emotional Technique). I listened to her for about half an hour, and then went home and looked it up on the Internet. Dr. Porter's website described NET as follows:

> Emotions are part of the natural, healthy response process we have to virtually every situation we encounter. However, sometimes challenging emotional experiences create lingering stress in our mind and body architecture. Such stress can contribute to physical and emotional difficulties. This technique is a powerful intervention that can assess and alleviate the internal stressors that are creating barriers to health.

I told Dad about it and then put it aside in my mind. I thought we'd been putting Diane through so much lately. Dad called me a few days later, to my surprise, and asked if I'd set up an appointment with Dr. Porter yet. I said I hadn't, but Dad thought, as I did, that NET made a lot of sense. Diane had always held in her emotions, and perhaps, as I'd said from the beginning, she had shut down because coping became too difficult. Her escape from this world and all the traumatic situations she'd gone through at work was Alzheimer's. Now, because Dad and I were taking care of every detail in her life, she no longer had to work or worry about anything.

Seeking A "Net"

We set up an appointment to see Dr. Porter, the chiropractic kinesiologist who specialized in NET, the following week. Dad, Diane, and I headed to yet another practitioner's office. We all really liked him. Dr. Porter used muscle testing and chiropractic techniques along with NET, and told us it would take many sessions to see any results. He put Diane in a machine that provided a baseline analysis of her body, and we got sobering news at our next visit: Diane's adrenal gland was very tired, her liver wasn't metabolizing properly, and her body wasn't able to properly digest calcium.

Dr. Porter put her on about 60 supplements a day and took her off the others her nutritionist and holistic doctor had her on for a while. He said her body was so out of whack that it was not able to process any of them properly. I didn't really understand how that could be—surely the other clinics would have realized this—but out of desperation I accepted things because there was nothing else to do.

I went to one session to observe. Dr. Porter first checked Diane's body alignment and then asked her several questions about her past while muscle testing her. Her body would tell him when he came across a bad memory and then he cleared it. It was all very interesting.

I asked him about something that had been puzzling me. Diane seemed to be able to converse much more easily after having a beer or glass of wine. Friends who attended parties at my house, where Diane might enjoy an alcoholic drink, had even commented that it seemed as though nothing was wrong with her. He was glad I shared that information with him, because it confirmed to him that her adrenal gland was tired. He said it's like kicking a sick horse (ugly analogy): it gets a little burst of energy and then it goes back to being sick. Alcohol, caffeine, and sugar all have this same effect on the adrenal gland—which had a lot to do with the circulation to the brain!

> 3 cups of coffee a day? The Journal of Alzheimer's Disease recently published a study that demonstrated some significant results related to coffee and cognitive function. The latest research presents even more compelling evidence of the possible benefits.—About.com

As the saying goes, you never know how and when things will come to you. I'd recently joined a new gym and was taking both weightlifting and Pilates classes. I hate gyms and always have; I'd joined a few and always quit because I didn't like being indoors. A new gym had opened around the corner from my house and my girlfriend Jodi talked me into joining. I thought it wouldn't hurt to do some cross-training, since all I did was run and do yoga, and perhaps it could be a nice social scene.

One night after Pilates class I walked out with a woman named Kate, who was Senior Director of Human Resources for Ceregene, a biotic company. I laughed and told her that most people who come into my life, even my clients, are associated with the biotech world. I then asked her what her company was working on and she said Alzheimer's! We talked in the parking lot until my teeth were chattering from the cold. She gave me her card and told me to visit the Ceregene website to read about their current Alzheimer's-focused project.

It turned out the study the Ceregene researchers were working on was being overseen by my least favorite doctor, Diane's Alzheimer's specialist, Dr. Thomas. They'd surgically implanted cells producing a nerve growth factor, which is a natural brain survival molecule, into the brains of Alzheimer's patients. The hope was that the implanted cells would prevent the death of some of the nerve cells affected by Alzheimer's disease and enhance the function of the remaining brain cells.

Here's another funny coincidence, even though they say there's no such thing. A few days later, Jodi and I were eating dinner at a local restaurant when two men in suits sat next to her. She began chatting with them and found out that they were famed doctors in San Diego for a conference. One was a heart surgeon and the other a brain surgeon. I'd just told Jodi about the Ceregene study, so she said I needed to talk to these guys about it. After they said yes to my polite request, I briefly told them about Ceregene, and they were both familiar with the study and the doctor doing it. They said he was brilliant and had been asked to speak at their conferences; there was a good chance the study was legitimate if he was working on it.

I was so excited I couldn't stand it. I wanted to get Diane into this program, and we had our third appointment with

Dr. Thomas in two weeks. When the day came, I launched into discussing this with him, but he cut me off, saying it was too early to tell if the implantation was working; researchers were only in the first testing phase and had no more money to continue the study. I felt my excitement being crushed, but then he said to ask him again in six months. Finally, new hope!

We did get some good news during that visit: Diane hadn't declined in the four months since he'd seen her. I asked if he thought she'd gotten any better. He said maybe a tiny bit; what did I think? I told him how Diane had mentioned she thought her writing had become a little easier, perhaps due to the mangosteen juice. He asked what mangosteen was and I knew I'd stuck my foot in my mouth. I started telling him about it, but he quickly stopped me because he didn't want to hear any more. He seemed to have blinders on when it had anything to do with nontraditional methods.

Shortly after this meeting we had a terrible blow. Dr. Thomas died! He was flying his small plane home from Palm Springs when he ran into bad weather and crashed into a mountain. My first thought was of how much this was going to affect the Alzheimer's Association, because he was the main man, but then it struck me that my chances of getting Diane into the study had crashed with him! I know it sounds terrible that I was only thinking of Diane and not his family in the wake of his death, but I'd become like a mother bear who would do anything for her cub.

Creating A Support Group

We decided to stop all Diane's holistic treatments because she was getting burned out with the whole process. Also, it was costing a fortune and nothing was really working. She seemed to be getting worse.

I was contacted by the Alzheimer's Association to see if we could use any help with Diane. I set up an appointment with our assigned counselor, who wanted Diane to participate in the "Out and About" group. Because she could no longer drive and thus didn't get out much, I thought it was a great idea. The program, run by the UCSD Alzheimer's Clinic, set up day trips for all the Alzheimer's patients to go to a bunch of great places. Dad only had to drop off Diane and pick her up a few hours later. She went once, discovered her "peers" were all about 70 years old, and said, "No way!"

Diane's UCSD counselor asked me why she didn't attend again. I used Diane's words to tell her that Diane "didn't want to hang out with a bunch of old people." I said she should let me know if a group was formed for people her age. I was really just joking, but within a few weeks she called to say they had eight people, all between the ages of 50 and 60, who'd recently been diagnosed with Alzheimer's. As a result of my comment—and Diane's reticence to join a group of "old people"—we started the first support group for early-onset Alzheimer's disease, and it involved both patients and their families!

The monthly gatherings, which Dad and I attended with Diane, were very helpful. Family members and Alzheimer's patients met in separate groups. It was good for the patients to be able to discuss what they were going through, but even more helpful for the caregivers to be able to share our experiences. In Diane's group there were two women around her age and four men. Diane was the only one still living on her own. In our group, Dad and I were the only ones who were not spouses, and we learned that the spouses had a more difficult time than we did. It was invaluable to talk with the husbands about what was going on with their wives so we could compare their stories to what Diane was going through.

One woman, Peggy, was at about the same stage as Diane. Peggy was like Diane in so many ways. They were about the same age and size, and Peggy had long curly gray hair. She was able to talk much more than Diane and was very funny, but Diane still had her wit and appreciated Peggy's. Peggy was a teacher and dancer—full of life when Alzheimer's hit her. I started contacting her husband, Michael, to compare stories. When he told me Peggy could no longer clean house, cook, dress herself, etc., it made me watch Diane a little closer.

One of the other women, Mary, was not as far along as Diane and Peggy. She'd just been diagnosed weeks before we had our first meeting. The three of them became buddies when they went on Out and About adventures together. I got to know Mary's husband, Gary, but I didn't talk to him as much as Michael, because Mary wasn't quite at the same level Diane and Peggy were.

Diane loved Out and About now. She'd really bonded with Peggy and Mary. Michael and I even arranged some personal play dates for them. To give Michael a little time to himself, I would meet him halfway so I could pick up Peggy for the day. I took her and Diane to the boardwalk in Mission Beach, where we walked a few miles and then ate lunch outside.

It was hard on these spouses who had to live with Alzheimer's every day. Dad and I felt fortunate and a little guilty that we each saw Diane just a few days a week. One night at a meeting, one wife/caretaker told us she had to put her husband in a home because he became violent with her; he'd gotten angry and broken a window with his fist. The men seemed to decline faster than the women in our group, and we speculated that might be because they were used to being the family breadwinners. Now that they had to be taken care of, it was a horrible blow to their egos.

At this time I also joined the Alzheimer's Gala Committee. I wanted to help with this annual fundraiser in some way. I ended up on the Acquisitions Committee, tasked with acquiring items for the event's silent auction. We met monthly for several months to get ready for the big night. Boy, did I feel out of place! The other ladies on the committee were professionals at raising money and some were on several boards. They were in a different category than I was. I'd never asked people to donate before, so it wasn't as easy for me.

At this point, the local NBC affiliate asked Diane and me to do a public service announcement (PSA) for Alzheimer's. Two other sets of people were doing the PSA with us; one was a couple we knew from the Out and About group, and the other a woman I met that day, who was there with her mother. The message was about how Alzheimer's can affect anybody: mothers, fathers, husbands, wives, brothers, and sisters. Diane and I sat next to each other on stools in the studio, and I explained how it affected us. We did several takes before I got it right, but I didn't see the finished product that day and I quickly forgot all about it.

We went to see Dr. Thomas' replacement, Dr. Radcliff, for Diane's six-month checkup. He was very young and quite nice. Diane had the same tests to track her progression. I told Dr. Radcliff I was going to be a thorn in his side because I'd been trying to get Diane into the Ceregene study for the cell implant surgery and the last thing Dr. Thomas had said to me was to ask him in six months. Dr. Radcliff said a new study was about to begin and they did need people for it. I was so excited! Finally some good news!

After Dr. Radcliff ran the tests, he sent Diane back to the waiting room and asked Dad and me back to his office to give us the results. Diane's score had now dropped too far to even qualify for the Ceregene program. I was devastated! That had been our only hope! What was I going to tell Diane? I'd promised I was going to get her into that program. I had no idea she'd declined so far so fast. As this news sunk in, I broke into tears again.

Several months later, my friend Kate at Ceregene called to tell me that she was very excited about the new test program being put together and thought we should try to get Diane in. I sobbed when I told her Diane was no longer eligible because the disease had progressed too far.

I told Kate about Mary from Diane's group and said because she was diagnosed much later than Diane, she was probably still eligible. I emailed her husband, Gary, who was like all of us at the beginning, so hopeful about beating this disease. He had Mary playing guinea pig at UCSD in the trials, but she was still going down the same road as the rest of the patients. I told Gary I knew exactly how he felt; we'd all been through the same process. We were always encouraged to participate in the most recent study, but in essence our family members were being used to develop a cure for the next generation because they were still so far away from one.

I told Gary the surgery Ceregene was doing was my last hope for Diane and I'd been fighting for it for a long time. It was now too late for her, but Mary might still have a chance. I very honestly told him I thought it was his last opportunity to do something we'd not done to see if it could save his wife.

After much research and thought, Gary decided to put Mary into the study and have the surgery. I was so nervous because I felt as though I'd talked him into it. I emailed Gary the day of the surgery, the day after the surgery, and several more times after that to see how Mary was doing. She'd gotten worse for a while and then kind of stabilized. No real change had occurred yet.

I know this sounds terrible, but while I felt let down for Gary and Mary, I also felt a little bit relieved knowing we didn't miss our chance of curing Diane with this procedure. Of course, there was a possibility that Mary hadn't been given the real cells, but a placebo. We'll never really know; that's the part about blind studies that really sucks!

One day at Diane's house, I noticed how thin she'd become and that none of the food I'd bought her the previous week had been eaten. As a test, I asked her to cook me breakfast and she just stared at me. I was seeing this look a lot lately, as if she just didn't quite know what you were saying to her. I then realized she no longer remembered how to use the microwave or the stove. We were told with Alzheimer's the mind would forget what hunger felt like, and she'd stop eating. Diane was also getting her drugs and vitamins all confused, and I was becoming very worried.

The Alzheimer's Association encouraged me to get Diane a Safe Return ID bracelet. In case she ever got lost, someone could help her get home safely by using the information engraved inside the bracelet. Diane had started walking around her own neighborhood now that she had to give up the beach walks, and I was worried she might become confused someday and not be able to find her way home. She was embarrassed at first by having to wear the ID bracelet and always made sure to also wear some decorative beaded bracelets to disguise it.

Diane loved to garden and I'd helped her plant flowers in her little patio for years. She loved to go to the nursery, pick out new flowers, and plant and care for them. One day I noticed after she planted all her flowers, the top inch of the roots was exposed. I told her if left that way, they'd dry out. When I suggested replanting them, she got very indignant, saying that was how Martha Stewart said to plant them. It was obvious Diane's confusion was getting worse.

Looking back at all of this now, I would have conducted some tests of my own on Diane much sooner than we did. I'd have given her a driving test a long time before she lost her license, a test to see if she could still use her appliances safely and cook for herself, and a test to see if she could walk around the block alone and find her way home. I was taking for granted that Diane was still able to function and live on her own, but she wasn't.

In hindsight, I really don't think Diane had been walking around the neighborhood all those months. I think she just told me she had so she looked competent, but she was probably too afraid of getting lost to actually do it. As I said before, Alzheimer's patients learn to put on a good front so they can keep their independence.

A Dramatic Change In My Life

It was around this time—two and a half years after Diane's troubles began—that my life really changed.

It all started on a Friday night when I left the salon after getting a new haircut. As all women have experienced, sometimes when you leave the chair you think you look fabulous, while other times you wonder what the heck the stylist was thinking. I was experiencing the latter emotion, so I decided to stop at the local Blockbuster and rent a good chick flick, cuddle up with the cats on the sofa with a glass of wine, and hide out for the evening.

As I was browsing the aisles for the perfect movie, Kate, my friend from Ceregene, called to ask if I'd meet her for a drink. I told her about my plans for the evening, the result of having a very bad hair night and looking very nerdy. She said she'd had a terrible day and would like to have a drink and talk. I told her I was right next door to Tuscany, our local bar and restaurant, and she should come over right away.

I really didn't like Tuscany because I thought it was kind of a pickup joint for older folks. I didn't want to go in on my own so I waited outside until Kate got there. Kate was a beautiful woman, about my age, 5'6", in great shape, and with a fun, short blonde haircut. Whenever we went anywhere together, men were immediately drawn to her. We sat at a table in the bar and had a bite to eat and a couple glasses of wine while I heard all about Kate's horrible day. We were thinking of leaving when a man approached our table and introduced himself to us. His name was Steve; he was 65, about 5'11" with sandy hair but not either of our types. Steve was very nice and interesting to talk to and before long we got onto the subject of "woo woo" stuff about the universe. I was totally into a deep conversation with him when I caught a glimpse of a man passing behind him who had deep, intense brown eyes— they were looking right into mine. My heart skipped a beat, which really surprised me because that hadn't happened in a very long time. A few minutes later he was at our table and Steve was introducing him to us as his friend RJ. I was thrilled that the man who'd caught my eye was actually talking to me! It got even better when I learned he was single; usually the guys I'm attracted to are married.

Before long the conversation came around to RJ's asking Kate and me how we knew each other. My heart stopped for a second and I thought, "Oh no, here we go again." I told him how we'd connected in a Pilates class, but then I learned Kate worked at Ceregene, which was conducting an Alzheimer's study I was trying to get my sister into.

The reason for my brief moment of anxiety was that in the years since Diane had been diagnosed, I'd not dated much, but the few dates I'd recently had went "running for the hills" the minute they discovered my sister had Alzheimer's and she was my responsibility. One of these quick-to-exit guys was even a prominent doctor, who clearly didn't have much compassion!

I was prepared for RJ to have a similar reaction, but after I shared Diane's story with him, he told me his daughter, Tylene, had worked in an Alzheimer's facility while going through college; she'd studied the brain for years and he suggested I talk to her. He wasn't scared off! This was encouraging. He asked me out to dinner the next night and called me every night after that. I guess my hair didn't look as nerdy as I thought!

On our first date I told RJ I was getting ready to turn 50 the following month. He told me he was 61, which shocked me because I thought he was maybe in his mid-50s! He looked so great; was tall (6'2"), which I love because I can wear all my four-inch heels; had those dark intense brown eyes that first drew my attention and a head of beautiful gray hair; and was in excellent physical shape. He went to the gym and worked out with weights a few times a week and it really showed—but what I was really attracted to was his brilliance.

I think it was our second date when RJ asked me where I wanted him to take me for my 50th birthday. I was a little surprised, because we were just getting to know each other, but by the sixth or seventh date we decided he could take me to Monterey for the big occasion. RJ treated me to the most wonderful getaway and spoiled me rotten. It had been a long time since I'd been treated so kindly and was with someone who wanted to take care of me.

RJ wasn't afraid of being around Diane and getting to know her. He'd go with us on Sunday adventures once a month or so. Diane announced at one of our early-onset Alzheimer's meetings, "Renae has a new boyfriend and I just love him!" She was so excited; she always greeted RJ with a long hug.

I was sad that RJ never got to meet Diane when she was her old self. I'd tell him stories about how funny and spunky she was. She was great at one-liners and getting in the first jab and usually the last as well. She was so quick-witted. I know they'd have really hit it off and probably been good sparring partners.

The night finally came for the big Alzheimer's Gala. All committee members were asked to volunteer in some capacity at the event. RJ and I signed up to work the registration desk. I thought this would be the most fun, because we could see all the famous local celebrities and the very wealthy as they entered. It was a formal affair, so RJ had gone shopping with me to pick out a dress and he was looking very handsome in his navy pinstriped suit.

This was the largest Alzheimer fundraiser of the year and all the elite of San Diego showed up; I think there were close to 400 people there. As the guests walked in, we got their names and gave them their packages with all the information about the silent auction items.

Once the silent auction portion was over, guests were asked to enter the main ballroom and find their seats for dinner and the presentation. All the volunteers would eat in the kitchen and we could hang out in the back of the ballroom to watch the festivities.

Suddenly, the head of our group asked me to follow her so she could seat RJ and me at a table. I said no, we didn't pay; we were just volunteers. She said she knew that, but she still wanted us to sit down. I was very confused but she sat us at a large round table right up front. Within a few minutes, all our tablemates started joining us. RJ said he'd never seen so many huge diamond rings in his life. We were sitting with a bunch of wealthy, elite San Diego women; RJ was the only man at the table. We couldn't figure out what the heck we were doing there.

When the ceremony started, a large screen was dropped into the middle of the room and a video started. There we were: Diane and I in the PSA. Oh my God! I'd totally forgotten all about it and had never seen it! Afterward, all of us in the video were asked to stand up, bright lights shined on us, and we got a wonderful ovation. What a night it turned out to be. Now I was the celebrity at the table. Everyone was so nice to us and we thoroughly enjoyed the live auction with these women. RJ and I could not believe the money they were spending that night—and it was all going to Alzheimer's.

In addition to prescribing Aricept to those who have symptoms of Alzheimer's, studies have shown by injecting B12 on a weekly basis the memory and overall cognitive functioning dramatically improved. Researchers discovered that deficient vitamin B12 levels correspond to both a decline in cognitive ability and a decrease in brain volume. Brain atrophy has been clearly identified as one of the physical effects of Alzheimer's disease.—About.com

We all realized Diane was getting to the point where she was in need of more assistance. This conversation was going to be a tough one! I brought it up to her one Sunday while we were out playing. "What would you think about having a roommate? Since you have two bedrooms, perhaps we could have someone move into your condo and help around the house. She could help you cook meals and take you wherever you wanted to go. I think it would be fun!" She said, "Absolutely not!" I'd expected this because she was so independent.

RJ was encouraging me to look into assisted living. His ex-mother-in-law had lived in a board and care facility he said was very nice; it was a private home that took in people who needed assistance without having to live in an actual "facility." I spent one whole day looking at board-and-care homes Diane could live in but they were just horrible! I came home in tears, saddened after seeing the poor choice of options. In all the homes I visited, the guests were sitting on sofas in front of a TV and, I suspect, heavily sedated. There was no way Diane was going anywhere like that! She wasn't quite ready for an Alzheimer's facility, but she needed something in between for now.

I was on the Internet looking at something related to work when I saw a pop-up ad for Atria Senior Living in Encinitas, so I called. I know there's no such thing as coincidence, but they said one room had just become available and encouraged me to take a look at it. I immediately hopped in the car and headed over there. It was only 12 minutes from me, so very convenient. It was one room with a bathroom and a small balcony that looked over a church playground; it was very pleasant.

I saw Diane the next day and mentioned the home to her, thinking she'd totally freak out like she did with the roommate idea. She must have known it was time. Perhaps she'd scared herself enough times already, because she just looked at me and said, "When can we go look at it?" Dad went with us to look at the place, and even though Diane looked really scared, she decided it was the thing to do. Thank goodness, Diane once again had put her trust in me to do the right thing for her—even though I wasn't even sure about this myself.

This next step was so difficult for me, and I'm sure it was even more painful for Diane, although she didn't show much emotion. I'd helped Diane design her little condo and it was just adorable. She'd collected antique furniture for 30 years, but only two end tables and a dresser could fit into her new space.

A few years earlier, I'd found her a beautiful Hepplewhite antique cherry dining table with six Chippendale chairs that would have to stay behind. She'd no longer have a kitchen, so everything in hers was left behind. I'd recently traded a friend some design hours for a suede sofa for Diane, but we couldn't take that either. Her guest room had a beautiful cherry desk I'd found for her, the twin bed we'd used as kids, and an old nightstand Dad had just repainted for her; all of it would be left behind.

Going through someone else's personal belongings, collections, and treasures to decide what could and couldn't be kept was excruciating. Diane had two large closets full of clothes but her new room only had space for about one-eighth of them. Under her stairway she had dozens of boxes of holiday decorations; I took a few small items for each holiday, so she could decorate her new space. I had to make decisions about artwork—what would adorn her new walls and what would have to stay. I was hoping we could rent out her condo furnished so we wouldn't have to get rid of any of her things, just in case. I was still forever hopeful.

This time is when I really fell in love with RJ. He'd become my rock when I had to make tough decisions. He was there, working elbow-to-elbow with Dad and me all day moving Diane into her new home. This was really the first opportunity he and my dad had to spend much time together. They both enjoyed making fun of me, teasing me by saying I was a control freak and enjoyed telling them what to do.

I'd measured all Diane's furniture and space planned her room so we'd only put things on the truck I knew would fit into the small space. When Dad or RJ suggested a piece of furniture go somewhere else than what I had on my floor plan, I'd just say, "No it has to go there." I did this with a smile, reminding them that space planning was one of my areas of expertise—how I made my living.

Early in the relationship, RJ warned me that I wouldn't wear the pants in the family. I chuckled to myself; I'd run my own life for 51 years and now this man is telling me he wants to wears the pants! I said, "Gladly, I'll drop them right now! I'm tired of having to wear them all the time!" That turned out to be easier said than done. I told him once that our relationship was like a "skort"; it looked like a skirt on the outside but there were pants underneath.

When we were finished, Diane's room was adorable and looked just like a miniature version of her house. My painter had painted the institutional white walls a buttery yellow, with the headboard wall painted a soft green. We took her antique nightstands and dresser, her bookcase, and her new brown velvet chair. I bought beautiful mahogany drapery poles and green linen drapery. We hung all her favorite pieces of artwork and threw down a new floral area rug over the not-so-attractive carpet. It was probably the prettiest room in the place!

We worked all day, and that evening when it was time to leave, it was excruciating for me to say goodbye to my lifelong friend, my sister. I gave her a long hug and asked if she was okay. "Yes," she said. I walked down the hallway as she stood in the doorway of her new room. I kept glancing back as she watched us all leave her, and saw she looked scared. Was I doing the right thing leaving her there?

Diane was the only person in the home who had Alzheimer's disease. Some of the guests were simply older and needed some assistance, while some were there temporarily, recovering from surgery. I had many conversations with the staff about Diane the day we moved her in. I let them know she had no concept of time, so they'd need to wake her up and get her for all meals as well as other activities. They were very accommodating and assured me she'd be fine.

I went to visit Diane the next day and discovered she'd actually settled in quite well. She said everyone there was really nice. Diane was a true people person and I think she realized this move could be a good thing. There was little for her to worry about—someone was watching over her all the time and someone always wanted to chat if she went down to the living room. She had three meals a day prepared for her, so we didn't have to worry about her remembering to eat, and the staff would give her all her meds, so we didn't have to worry about her getting them confused anymore.

I actually teased her about her new living arrangement. "You're such a princess. You have your room cleaned for you, your laundry done for you, all your meals cooked for you, someone who pays all your bills, and a chauffeur! I want to move in here!"

After learning we wouldn't be able to rent out Diane's condo furnished, Dad, RJ, and I cleaned it out and donated everything we couldn't fit into her new residence. I'd been concerned that I might not be doing the right thing by moving her out of her condo, but when we started going through her things, I knew it was the right time, if not a little late. It was very apparent that she'd been living in confusion for some time.

People who may be in the early stages of Alzheimer's disease can experience one or more of these symptoms in different degrees:

Memory loss that disrupts daily living
Challenges in planning or problem solving
Difficulty completing usual tasks at home or work
Confusion with time, seasons or place
Trouble understanding visual images (colors and shapes) and spatial relationships (distances)

New problems using words in speaking and writing
Misplacing things and losing the ability to retrace steps
Decreased or poor judgment
Withdrawal from work or social activities
Changes in mood or personality—Alz.org

RJ was right by my side once again. It's an uncomfortable and strange feeling to go through someone else's personal things and toss most of them out. At this time I had a talk with my dad, saying that going through this once was quite enough for me; I didn't want to do it again with his personal belongings. He was approaching 79, had a large house that was stuffed full, a barn, and a 37-foot motor home filled with more stuff, plus rental property. I told him it was up to him to start downsizing and getting rid of all his stuff. He snickered; he'll probably make me do it all!

Dad wanted to put Diane's condo up for sale. This freaked me out and I asked him to hang onto it for a while. I don't know if I was still thinking Diane was going to recover and I wanted her to know she still had her home if she wanted to move back. The housing market had dropped so much in 2007 that Dad wouldn't get much for it anyway, so I convinced him to rent it out. He listed it on Craig's List and was contacted by Diane's friend Heather, who asked if she and her mom could rent it. Perfect!

Diane just loved Heather and her mom, Pam, so she was thrilled that they'd be living in her home. Years ago, when Diane was still at the TV station, Heather had a brain tumor and ended up having brain surgery. She wasn't fully functional while recovering and had no idea she should have been completing the paperwork required to collect disability insurance. Heather was in a real bind when she was left unable to work and she also couldn't drive because of vertigo.

When I learned of her predicament, I offered to assist with the paperwork in any way I could, since I'd done it for Diane. I was pretty sure I could have helped her, but she never asked for my assistance. I felt bad that I hadn't done more to help her, but I did have a pretty full plate at the time.

I think it's an odd coincidence that Diane and Heather both ended up with brain issues.

As I drove around and saw homeless people, I always wondered if they had medical issues and fell between the cracks. It would be so easy to end up on the streets if you didn't have family to help you. I thought of how difficult it was for me to do all the paperwork that needed to be done for Diane over the years. Can you imagine if you had a mental issue that wouldn't allow you to do the due diligence it takes to get a check from the government to survive if something happened to you? It's something our society needs to deal with in a more humane and helpful way, and best done early in the process!

Most of the guests at Atria were very sharp and took Diane under their wings, watching over her. The staff told me some of the guests thought Diane was a spy, since she was certainly too young to be living in a senior home at 53.

By this time it was difficult for Diane to speak, but the staff and the other residents were very kind to her. She told me shortly after she moved in that it was the best thing I could have done for her. Wow! I really needed to hear that.

It was great for me as well, because Diane was now so close to me that I could stop by anytime without getting on the freeway and fighting the traffic; I was able to spend more time with her. Instead of just devoting one whole day to her, I could also stop by to say hi, and sometimes stay for a short visit if I was driving by. These short visits did have a hitch, however, because she was so used to me taking her for the day whenever I saw her that she didn't understand why I'd stop by and then leave her there.

Later that month, RJ took me to Sonoma on a wine trip with 15 of his friends. We arrived a day before everyone else and checked into the Ledson Hotel, which overlooked the park in the town center. The place was absolutely beautiful! The rooms were all designed differently and appeared to be turn-of-the-century, but were actually only a few years old. They had inlaid wood floors and ornate marble-top vanities in the dressing area; gorgeous furniture, bedding, and drapery; and to top it off, large bathtubs with chandeliers hanging over them in the small alcove next to the bed. Very romantic!

We opened a bottle of wine, which had been left in our room as a gift, and sat on our balcony enjoying the park view. Later, we had dinner in a wonderful restaurant and then went next door to have an after-dinner drink at a little bar—where RJ asked me to marry him! He had this all planned and I was totally clueless!

I was dealing with so much at this point in my life that something like this was the farthest thing from my mind. I said yes, but hardly slept the entire night. Life had been so stressful and hectic; all I could think about was whether I'd need to move, or would he. Where were we going to live: my place or his?

The next morning room service knocked at the door and RJ asked me to get it. They delivered a beautiful bouquet of flowers with a card addressed to Mrs. Pommer. I guess he assumed I'd say yes.

I later asked him if it would hurt his feelings if I kept my name, because I'd had it for 51 years. My company was in my name and I really liked my name. He said he hadn't told them to put Mrs. Pommer on the card and never assumed I'd change my name.

That morning, as I was meeting RJ's friends over breakfast, we announced that we become engaged the night before. The weekend became a three-day wine-tasting celebration of our engagement!

Then we had to decide where we'd get married. I'd never wanted a big wedding, so I suggested we just have family and a few friends attend a ceremony at one of the wineries in Sonoma. When I got home and started telling all my friends, they were disappointed they couldn't be there, too. One said, "You can't wait until you're 51 to get married and then just run off and not throw a big party!"

Claudia, my sister-in-law's sister, called to make sure that we were getting married in her backyard. I remembered then that after attending her wedding and her son's wedding, both in their backyard, I'd said if I ever did get married, I wanted to get married there, too.

She and her husband, Jack, had just planted a vineyard in the upper parcel of their property. I told RJ about it and asked him to meet me at the house because he'd never seen it before. He quickly agreed.

Jack and Claudia's backyard is an adult version of Disneyland. It's the most beautiful place you can imagine. Claudia is somewhat of a professional entertainer. She had special events at the house frequently, so she became my wedding planner and took over the whole affair. I didn't need to do a thing except select the food with her caterer and be somewhat involved with the choice of music together with her DJ. I did buy my dress, of course, but Claudia graciously did everything else.

It's funny that I'm such a control freak in so many ways, especially with my interior design work, but when it came to the duties involved with my wedding, I released most of them to Claudia without a second thought.

On May 10, 2008, we were married. I didn't meet my husband in Tuscany the countryside as I'd imagined, but I did meet him in Tuscany the restaurant. I love that story! You have to be so clear when you're making those visualizations! We didn't get married in a vineyard in Tuscany, but we did get married in a vineyard in Jack and Claudia's backyard in Olivehain, California.

It was a beautiful wedding! Over 100 people were there; my dear friend Jackie married us; and Diane and my sister-in-law, Trudy, were my maids of honor. Trudy walked down the aisle with Diane, holding her hand. It was wonderful.

Diane had always dreamed of my getting married. It was much more important to her than it ever was to me. I was thrilled she was so excited when I told her and she understood I wanted her and Trudy to be my maids of honor because I'd served in that capacity for both of them.

I'm so happy Diane was able to be in my wedding photos, but it makes me a little sad whenever I look at them and see her eyes; they were always unfocused and looking in a different direction instead of at the camera.

To make things even more wonderful, my dad was married two weeks before me, so we had them join us for the first dance at our wedding. It was a whirlwind romance. Dad had gone back to Jamestown, North Dakota, for, as we joked, a class reunion for anyone who was still alive. Dad was 78.

He re-met a woman he had a crush on in eighth grade, Margie Lee, who'd been my mom's high school roommate. (When you lived on a farm, you had to move into town when you started high school.) Margie had kept in touch with my mom until she died in 1976, so she knew all about everyone in the family until that time.

At the time of the reunion, Margie's husband, Clayton, had been gone for 13 years, and she hadn't had anyone special in her life since. Margie was still a schoolteacher, and she spent most of her spare time with her grandchildren, who just adored her. Dad and Margie hit it off and started emailing back and forth; the following summer, Dad went back to visit her and meet her family.

They'd fallen in love, but Margie didn't want to leave her family and my dad was "no way" going to move back to North Dakota! No more snow for him. A few days after he drove home alone, she called him and had decided, after much thought, to leave her four kids and her grandchildren and start her life again in San Diego with Dad. It was her turn to live and she realized her family would survive without her.

The first time we all met Margie she'd just moved to San Diego and we had lunch at the Chart House, a beachfront restaurant—a far cry from North Dakota! I could see why Dad fell in love with her. She was adorable, about 5'6" with olive skin, dark eyes, and brown hair with a little touch of salt, and she had a beautiful smile and laugh. She was so appreciative of everything that had happened to her—especially finding Dad and living in San Diego. She was like a little kid in her enthusiasm. She and Dad had so much in common even though he hadn't lived in North Dakota for 52 years. They knew all the same people, they were raised with a small-town mentality, and they have the same life values.

Not long after Margie moved west, she and Dad were married at their church in a small ceremony with just their best friends as witnesses.

We were all so glad Margie changed her mind about leaving her family in North Dakota. We love her and they're just adorable together. What a blessing they fell in love and got married at 78! It was so special that Dad and I both found love at the same time in our lives.

Diane Meets Abdon

Next comes the most unexpected love story of all, as if Dad's and mine weren't surprising enough!

The day we were walking Diane through Atria the first time, when we were standing in the dining room, Abdon, an Atria employee, came in and saw her. Later, he told me his first thought was, "Damn, that's a beautiful lady!" He said he never could have imagined there was anything wrong with her; he assumed we were checking out the place for our mother, father, or other elderly family member. He said he fell in love with her the minute he saw her.

Abdon drives the Atria bus that takes residents wherever they need to go, so he knows everyone who lives there. He kept seeing Diane around and wondered what she was doing there. At first he thought she was the daughter of someone who lived at Atria and was just visiting. Finally he asked one of the nurses who she was and he learned Diane was a resident. He couldn't believe it! He asked what her problem was and found out she had Alzheimer's. Abdon said, "It broke my heart, right then and there. How can that be? It's not fair! I really started fighting with my feelings of what life is all about."

A few weeks later, Abdon noticed Diane hadn't been participating in any activities. He asked a staff member why she wasn't joining in and was told she didn't want to—but the fact was, she was unable to do most of them. Abdon asked if it was okay for him to take Diane on his bus. He'd not even talked to her yet.

I ran into Abdon around this time and he asked if I knew anything about Aricept. I had to chuckle to myself because he was so cute and trying to be helpful. I let him know we'd been battling this for quite a few years already, and I did know about Aricept, but I thanked him anyway.

Abdon was so sweet; he was 53, Diane's age, and 5'4", her height. He was Hispanic, with a very cute accent, a great smile, and a very free laugh. He was very funny and had a great since of humor, which I knew Diane would appreciate.

When Abdon asked me if it would be okay if he started taking Diane on the bus with him while he was driving the other guests around, I asked her what she thought. She walked over to Abdon and put her head on his shoulder! I guess that meant it was okay with her.

Abdon was a little embarrassed when she did this and started looking around at the rest of the staff, wondering what they would think. Gary, the manager, was standing there, too. Abdon said he hoped they didn't get the wrong idea, because he didn't even know Diane. He was very surprised by her response. I think Diane was following her intuition.

Every day after that, Abdon would pick up Diane from her room and walk her down to the bus. She'd ride with him until it was time to come back and eat lunch, and then go back on the bus for the rest of the day. She enjoyed the view from the bus and would point out things she saw to Abdon. He said she didn't talk much, but he could tell she was enjoying herself. Just being able to see the outside world and not be stuck inside her room had to be a very pleasant change in her daily life.

Abdon said he started flirting a little with her on the bus. "I could sense there was something there by the way she looked at me. I wasn't sure if this was right, but I'm sorry, this was how I felt about her." He'd see her staring at him in the rearview mirror and when he looked back she'd look down. "One time I threw her a little kiss through the rearview mirror and she blushed. Another day when I was dropping her off at her room and saying goodbye, I don't know why but I decided to give her a little kiss on the cheek—but she moved and I kissed her on the lips instead, and I thought, oh shoot!"

Abdon was not expecting it, but he could tell their feelings for each other were getting stronger. One day she got on the bus and Diane said, "Hi honey!" He looked around and asked himself, "Is she talking to me?" She was, and there were other people on the bus who heard what she said.

The first time I really heard about their relationship was when I went to pick up Diane from one of her Out and About trips at another senior center. Through Atria, I'd arranged to have Abdon drop her off and I'd pick her up. One day she came out holding a single red rose. I asked where she'd gotten it and she said Abdon had given it to her.

After that, I'd often see a single red rose in a vase sitting on her dresser. When I'd ask who gave it to her, she'd always grin and say, "Abdon." He usually brought her candy as well. She'd save the Werther's Originals because she knew Dad and I like those.

Back in the old days, whenever anyone went to Diane's house, a bowl of candy was always sitting on her dining room table, usually chocolate because a day without chocolate was not worth living according to Diane. Now we always made sure Diane had a bowl of candy on her dresser—a taste of home, so to speak. Those who visited her enjoyed it, as did the staff.

One day Abdon told me he bought her two little stuffed animals. "I said the little pink poodle was her and the Chihuahua was me, but she wouldn't take them." Abdon started laughing while he was telling me this story. "She said she didn't have room for them." He brought it up several months later and asked if she remembered turning down the little stuffed dogs he'd tried to give her and she said, "Yes, I was a bitch." Who knew what that was all about? Abdon and I tried to figure it out. Was it because it meant something about them being a couple and she just wasn't ready for that, or did she think I, as her interior designer, wouldn't approve of them in her décor?

Diane hadn't been in a relationship for about 18 years. After her marriages and long cohabitation, she decided she liked being single. For the past 5 years, of course, just getting well and fighting her disease had been her priority.

Diane had pretty much sworn off men. When Abdon first met her and asked if she had a boyfriend, she said, "No, no more boys!" Abdon wasn't put off. "What about me?" he asked. "I'm not a boy. I'm a man. I'm a macho man." Diane laughed; he could always make her laugh. He laughs a lot and his laughter is quite contagious.

People have this perception that either you get Alzheimer's or you don't. But there's actually more of a sliding scale of brain health as you age and a lot depends on genetics and lifestyle together. If everyone in the U.S. adopted just one positive habit, like getting regular exercise or learning to manage stress, within five years we could expect 1 million fewer Alzheimer's cases. When you get your heart to pump more blood, it sends more oxygen and nutrients to the brain.—Dr. Gary Small, author of *The Alzheimer's Prevention Program.*

I was looking for someone to take Diane out for walks a few days a week so Dad didn't have to drive 45 minutes to Encinitas two or three times a week to walk with her. When Abdon heard about that, he volunteered, saying he needed to lose some weight. He and Diane started walking after he got off work. Gary saw them walking one evening, holding hands. He told Abdon it was okay for Diane to walk with her arm through his, but he probably shouldn't hold her hand. It just didn't look proper.

Who would have thought Diane would find a boyfriend living at a senior home and fighting Alzheimer's!

Abdon's evening walks with Diane eventually turned into taking her out to dinner. Being such a gentleman, he called and asked my permission before he did. This thrilled me! Abdon was so polite. He was a retired Marine with six children of his own, and a real caregiver. He was an angel to take Diane so thoughtfully into his life.

Abdon shared some of his life story with me, telling me that eight years after he retired from the Marines, he decided to fulfill a long-time dream of volunteering in a senior center. He thought this was something he would really enjoy, so he became a Certified Nurse Assistant.

Abdon said, "I saw how difficult a job it was both physically and mentally, but I loved it. I hardly ever had time to have lunch. I'd take a 10- to 15-minute break to have a snack and then get back to the residents. I loved the way the residents

I was assigned to would say 'thank you for being so nice to me' and they really meant it. I thought they didn't know the difference between someone who cared about them or not, but they did. They were very much aware of their needs. I loved the work but it was very hard, because I got too attached to residents and didn't know if I should be. I spoke to some of my coworkers about it and they told me I was fine; this is how it should be. I did it for about three years, but I didn't like not having enough time to devote to each resident, so even though it broke my heart, I stopped working as a CNA."

One night I was dropping off Diane after taking her out to dinner. I'd always check her answering machine because she couldn't any more. There was a message from Abdon saying goodnight and he ended the message with "I love you." I looked at Diane and told her that he said he loves you. She replied yes, and she loved him, too.

Abdon saw Diane first as a friend. "I thought if I was ever going to be a friend to someone, she would be it. The first year we were dating she didn't talk very much, but I always felt we were on the same wavelength. We were just happy being with each other and it eventually turned from friendship to love."

On weekends, Abdon would check out Diane for adventures. He'd take her to the zoo one weekend and the wild animal park the next. Diane had a yearly membership at the San Diego Zoo for years and went often. Abdon said her long-term memory would kick in and she'd grab his hand and take him around. He'd never been there so had no idea where to go, but Diane led the way. One day he took her on the Midway aircraft carrier, where visitors use headphones to take walking tours. Another time he took her to Medieval Times, which she remembered; she'd try to tell Abdon when things were going to happen in the show.

Abdon bought her a photo album and started filling it with the pictures he took of her that day. One day he took her to Tijuana, put a sombrero on her, and sat her on a zebra, which was really a donkey painted with black and white stripes; what a picture that was. I'd look at the album every week when I went to visit and she'd try to explain what they did over the weekend. The photo of her on the zebra cracked me up because somewhere we had that same picture of Diane when she was just four or five years old.

Abdon had several family members living in Pasadena, and one day he took Diane to meet them. His oldest daughter, Christy, questioned Abdon about dating Diane. She said, "Oh Dad, you're going to get hurt!" Abdon replied, "Yes, I know, but I don't care. I can't stop loving her because of what's going to happen to her. I've got to love her and then whatever happens, happens." Christy understood; she was mature enough to allow Abdon to live his own life.

Diane tried to tell me about his family but she used very few words at this time. All she could say was, "They are so nice. They treat me so nice." She showed me pictures of them in the photo album. Abdon said, "My family just accepted her. They didn't ask me questions about her and no one mentioned her situation; they just went along. They saw how happy I was with Diane, so that was all that mattered to them."

Abdon took Diane to the Rose Bowl Parade. For 20 years while helping with Thanksgiving dinner, she and I had talked about how one day we were going to volunteer to work on the floats in a parade and then attend the parade. We'd always say, "Next year!" Diane loved parades. She watched the Macy's Thanksgiving Day Parade and the Rose Bowl Parade every year. I was so thrilled that she finally had the opportunity to experience it firsthand! She had lots of pictures in her photo album to share this special day with me. Abdon hadn't even known that was one of her dreams. I asked Abdon if he was scared when he first started "dating" Diane: "You do know what Alzheimer's disease is, don't you?" He answered, "I'm not scared, but I do dread the ending. I wasn't scared during our relationship since it started as a friendship. I didn't care about what happened on a daily basis or the problems it created with all the other residents resenting her being on the bus all the time, or the problems I might have created with Gary. I just didn't care about it. This is the way I feel about her and whatever happens, happens."

Before long, Abdon was calling to ask my permission to check out Diane for weekends to spend more time at his house in Escondido; it was a long drive back and forth for him otherwise. Because theirs wasn't an "appropriate relationship," I'd go to Diane's on Friday afternoon, pack a suitcase for her, and check her out for the weekend—and then rendezvous down the street with Abdon and turn her over to him. After a while, people started to just ignore what was going on and Abdon got the staff to pack her suitcase. He'd then sneak her down the back stairway, which was right next to her room. It was all a big adventure for Diane!

One day I took Diane out to lunch and she was trying to tell me what they'd done the past weekend; she said they just hung around and watched movies at his house. I asked her if she and Abdon were having sex. She got a funny grin on her face and said yes. I was so excited for her; it had been years! I asked how it was and she said it was good. She wasn't able to give many details but that was okay. Just the look on her face told me how happy she was.

Diane couldn't take part in most of the activities offered at the senior center because of her Alzheimer's—she couldn't do the art classes, she couldn't play games, and she was too physically fit to do their exercise classes, which consisted of sitting in a chair—so when Abdon decided to put her on his bus every day, she blossomed. She thought this was her new job and looked forward to helping Abdon with all the old people on the bus.

On one of the days I took her on her favorite beach walk, she stopped about halfway through and said she should get back because she needed to be on the bus to help Abdon. He needed her help. At first my feelings were hurt a bit, but I soon realized it was fine if she'd rather be with him.

Unfortunately, this situation started a big scandal at Atria. Apparently, there was unrest because the other residents didn't understand why Diane was getting so much of Abdon's attention and a bit of jealousy had raised its ugly head. Older people (in this case, women) can be extremely judgmental. Gary ultimately told Abdon that Diane was no longer permitted to ride on the bus the entire day with him. This news broke my heart.

I went in to have a talk with Gary. He was a really nice guy but he was trying to keep his job and the whole thing with Diane and Abdon dating had become a big issue. I don't think management had ever had to deal with this kind of problem before, and it was a bit funny when you think about it.

I told Gary this was a very special case. Diane and Abdon were in love and we didn't really have any right to interfere because they were both adults. I explained this was Diane's only real pleasure in life. All the other residents could read, play games, and participate in group discussions and exercise classes, but Diane couldn't do any of those things. Her biggest joy was being able to ride around on the bus with Abdon. Gary was empathetic, but said he had to be very careful because they were crossing the line.

I joked with Diane about always having to be the troublemaker. When she was young, she was often in trouble at school for being boy crazy. She usually got bad grades for talking too much with the boys in the back of the room, and she was still causing trouble with the boys! She'd just laugh.

One day when I was visiting Diane, a lady grabbed my arm and asked if I was Diane's sister. I said I was, and she went into an angry rampage! She was very upset that Diane had been kicked off the bus and wanted to do something about it. I told her I'd been trying, to no avail. I said I wanted to get a petition together, but my husband told me I should lay low so we didn't get Abdon fired. She said she wanted to do it. She asked if I'd type up something for her and she'd take it around and get the necessary signatures. She was a hoot! I got her name, June, and her room number. I went home, typed up the petition, and slipped it under her door a few days later.

A week or so after that, June called to tell me that she had several signatures from residents who wanted Diane back on the bus, too. June marched the petition into Gary's office and demanded Diane be allowed back on the bus! She told him Diane shouldn't have to suffer just because of a couple of fuddy duddies at Atria. Long story short, June got Diane back on the bus! She was my hero.

June and I talked for quite a while the evening of her triumph and at the end of our conversation, I told her how great she was and how I just loved her spunk! She said, "That's what got me to my age," which was 96! I was impressed. The way she looked and spoke made me think the oldest she could be was maybe 80. What an angel! Diane had many people watching over her there. They all felt so sorry for her having this horrible disease at such a young age. I think it made them all feel a little bit grateful, even though they were declining physically, that they still had their minds.

Once the process that destroys brain cells has begun, the disease is irreversible.—Alz.org

Having Abdon come into our lives right then was a godsend. We welcomed him into our family and he fit right in. Because Dad and I had both just been married and felt we needed to devote time to our new spouses, we were now able to do so and not feel guilty. Now all three of the Farleys were in love. Who would have ever imagined it! It really was a fairy tale.

Diane and Abdon's relationship was really remarkable, especially because Diane made sure Abdon didn't feel like a caretaker. He said, "She was always the one trying to take care of me. She was always worried about me. She was always worrying about everyone else but herself." I could relate to this, because when Diane was first diagnosed she was upset and said, "I'm the big sister. I'm supposed to take care of you, not the other way around."

When Diane had been at Atria for only a few months, one of the male residents inappropriately touched one of the female residents. Diane was in a group of all the women talking about it. She was very upset and said she'd take care of this guy. She'd beat him up! Abdon told her to calm down; she was a lady. Diane said she didn't care—she could do it! And I knew she could, because she could be a little toughie when she wanted to.

It was now the holidays and RJ and I had everyone over for Christmas Eve dinner. Rick called from Hawaii right when we sat down to eat. After we passed the phone around and everyone talked to him for a bit, Abdon said he and Diane would love to go to Hawaii. I told him if he wanted to take her I'd pay the airfare and they could stay with Rick and Trudy, so it would be pretty inexpensive. He was so excited he couldn't stand it! He told everyone at Atria that they were going to Hawaii!

I was excited, too. I'd always taken Diane on all her adventures. She hadn't been on one vacation in the past 18 years that wasn't with me. She wasn't one to plan a trip, but always wanted to go with me whenever I needed a travel buddy. Lately I'd been feeling guilty traveling with RJ because she wasn't able to go. Taking her anywhere had become very difficult.

Diane and Abdon had a wonderful time in paradise, and it was great for Rick and Trudy to be able to spend some time with Diane. I told Rick it might be the last time she knew who he was, because she was declining quite quickly by then. Abdon took lots of pictures and put them in Diane's photo album when they returned.

When they got back, I asked Abdon about the trip and whether it was difficult for him because Diane's Alzheimer's was getting so much worse. He said he had to handle all the luggage himself and she'd often get confused, but he did fine. "For the most part it went okay. She trusted me, so she'd just follow along. However, one day she got really upset with me because I dressed her in something she didn't like. She always wanted to look pretty and she didn't like the way she looked. She got upset when I tried to put capri pants on her because her legs weren't shaved, so I had to shave her legs."

Diane would tell me about their time together, saying Abdon was the best man she'd ever been with. I was so excited for her. All I'd ever wanted was for her to find a good man who really appreciated her for who she was. None of the other relationships she'd had were with men like Abdon. Who'd have imagined Diane would find the love of her life now? And Abdon felt the same about her.

Abdon saw the true essence of Diane even through her disease. He told me he was glad he met her when he did because if their paths had crossed before, she probably wouldn't have looked twice at him. If that were true, she would have missed out on someone really exceptional.

Shortly after this, I took Diane out to lunch and told her I'd just talked to Rick. Diane said she wanted to go to Hawaii. I was startled and told her she'd just returned from there! She didn't remember going, so when I took her back to her room, I pulled out her photo album and showed her the pictures Abdon had taken of their trip. Her eyesight was getting progressively worse and she really had a hard time focusing on the pictures. Then she became upset because she couldn't remember the trip.

One day when I went to pick up Diane, she looked like she hadn't washed her hair in weeks! She said she did that morning, but I realized what had happened. She wasn't washing the shampoo or conditioner out of her hair, so it just looked greasy. I washed her hair again and blow-dried it before we went out for the day. She'd stopped wearing makeup—she'd forgotten how to put it on—so I dolled her up a little before we went out.

Diane now needed more help getting ready in the morning, and I asked the staff to include that as part of their daily routine. They needed to wake her up, shower and dress her, and deliver her to Abdon for her bus ride every day.

When Diane was first diagnosed, she'd come to my place for the weekend and we'd go to the beach, where I'd run and she'd power walk for an hour. We'd meet at the end and go to breakfast. I'd always ask her as I left her in the parking lot where she was going to walk. She'd get embarrassed by this, but said "the park." She knew when she got to the park she was to turn around and walk back.

One day as I was putting on her hat and zipping up her sweatshirt—something else that embarrassed her because she couldn't do it on her own anymore—I asked her the same question. She just looked at me, couldn't figure out the word for park, and said "green."

I always knew where I'd pass her on my run back, but one day she wasn't there. I got worried; my adrenaline kicked in, and I sped up until I got back to the parking lot, where I found her. When I asked how she beat me back she couldn't answer. I think she got confused and never made it to the park. I tried to have a run/walk outing one more time after that, and Diane did get lost. I found her walking back and forth on the path, but she'd never made it to the park. I felt horrible to think I could have lost her. I always gave her the benefit of the doubt when perhaps I shouldn't have.

We started walking together after that. Her eyesight was getting even worse and one day she tripped and fell after failing to see a curb, bloodying the palms of her hands. She was most worried about the beaded bracelet that helped disguise her Alzheimer's ID bracelet; it had broken and the beads were rolling down a hill. She wanted to pick them up and remake the bracelet, but I convinced her she had a similar bracelet at home. I felt terrible. When I later explained to Abdon about her hands, he told me I should be holding onto her arm when we walked because she really wasn't able to see well and was also becoming a little unsteady.

It wasn't long after they returned from Hawaii that Abdon asked if he could come over to the house to talk. I knew what was coming. Abdon, RJ, and I sat in our living room and he told us Diane really needed more help than he thought she could get living at Atria; it wasn't set up to take care of Alzheimer's patients. He said his job had become very difficult because Diane had become so dependent on him, and he thought it was best for her if she moved into a designated Alzheimer's home.

He also said he thought he needed to start distancing himself from her because it was getting so hard for him. Abdon later said, "I hated to tell you this, but I realized it was getting more and more difficult for me. I was upset because no matter how much I wanted to help her, I couldn't. I realized no matter how much I did with her, or for her, she wasn't really there anymore. And it was breaking my heart."

We cried together and I told Abdon how lucky Diane was that he'd been there to love her for the past year. We let him know we were all so grateful to him and we truly understood; we were thankful for the times he was there for her.

At that time I put this book aside. I could see we weren't going to be able to turn off this ugly disease. It was going to run its course no matter what we did and there was just nothing more we could do. The title of this book was originally going to be My Sister's Recovery from Alzheimer's. Diane's recovery wasn't going to happen, so I saw no point in continuing to write.

Shortly after that, I met a girlfriend for happy hour at the new hotspot in town, 333 Pacific. We were sitting at a long table in the middle of the bar when two men came and sat across from us. At first I was disappointed because I just wanted to catch up with my friend and we certainly weren't there to meet men. However, as they started talking to us, I found out one of them was a writer who'd published several books. I told him I'd been writing a book but just scrapped it. When he asked what the book was about, I briefly explained the situation to him.

His first reaction was, "You have to finish this book!" I replied that I couldn't get the ending I wanted, but he told me that didn't matter. He said I could change the title of the book; it was still a great story people would want to read. I don't know this man's name, but I'm grateful he gave me this advice, or you wouldn't be reading Diane's story right now.

Not long after that, while on one of my beach runs, it came to me. I could turn the book into a love story about Diane and Abdon, which really was the most amazing part of everything that happened. It could still have "a happy ending."

I was disappointed when I learned Oprah would be ending her talk show. I'd planned to send my book to her and dreamed of it being one of her monthly book club recommendations. I'd imagined myself being a guest on her show and giving everyone in the audience a copy of my book. Oh well, I knew all too well that all dreams don't come true.

Moving Into The Manse

About a year and a half after we moved Diane into Atria, shortly after our conversation with Abdon, I spent an entire day researching all the Alzheimer's homes that would take Medicare. RJ and I spent one whole Sunday going to all the homes on my list, and a few that weren't on it. All the really nice ones were at least $7,000 to $8,000 a month, and they didn't take Medicare. We just couldn't afford that—and I'd never let her step foot in the homes we could afford. I came home totally depressed.

Diane was getting about $2,200 a month from Social Security disability and she was running out of the money she'd saved in her retirement savings account. Dad, Rick and Trudy, and I all knew we'd have to start chipping in when her funds ran out.

The following Monday I started searching on the Internet and then remembered I'd been contacted a long time ago by an agency that helps place family members in situations like ours. I called and the phone was answered by a woman with the voice of an angel. I was so emotional I started crying as I told her I needed to find a nice place for my sister but we couldn't afford what the nice places were asking. In a very sweet, angelic voice, she said, "Don't you worry. I'll find something for your sister and call you back." I believed her and she did. Within a few hours she sent me to the website of a place in Vista. I immediately set up an appointment and went to check it out that afternoon.

The place was only about 10 minutes from our house, so that was good. I drove down a long driveway and ended up at a wrought iron gate, and what stood behind it was a huge colonial mansion! It was a white two-story house with Doric columns, a red brick façade, and green shutters. A tall, white stone water fountain with a woman in the center, like something you'd see in Rome, sat in the middle of the circular drive. I thought this couldn't be right! I rang the bell and waited until someone opened the gate.

The house was called The Manse. A very wealthy doctor owned it many years ago; he'd owned most of the surrounding area as well. Across the street there'd been a large tennis court and on the side was an old abandoned indoor pool, which I imagine was really something back in its day.

When the doctor's wife was diagnosed with Alzheimer's disease and he was unable to find a suitable place for her, he decided to convert his own 21-bedroom mansion into an Alzheimer's home.

I walked through the big white double doors and was taken upstairs to meet the current owner. She took me on a tour of the place, which was decorated very "cutesy country." There was a center courtyard with lots of sunshine and flowers and a swing bench. It was all very nice until we went into the main living room where all the guests were, and then reality hit me. The residents were all sitting on the sofa in front of a TV and most of them were sleeping. My worst nightmare! She said she only had one room available and it wasn't in the main house, but in the detached guesthouse with three other women. I thought that sounded great after touring the main house, which was too depressing.

We walked next door to the guesthouse, and it was simply charming. It had a shared living room with white wicker furniture and a TV. It had one shared bathroom, which was OK because Diane needed assistance with showering now anyway. When we entered the available room, it was being painted the same color green I'd painted one of the walls in Diane's room at Atria. It was a bit smaller, but it was within our price range! What a miracle!

Then came the hard part; I had to tell Diane she was moving. She'd been so sweet and cooperative up to this point and would always say she'd do anything I told her to do because she knew I was always looking out for her best interests. Now, when she found out she'd no longer be seeing Abdon on the bus every day, she was very upset.

Diane would not look at me or speak to me. She said she wasn't going to move. I finally got a little harsh with her because I didn't know what else to do. I said I was sorry, but her life was in my hands and this was the best I could do for her right now. I told her I'd spent days looking for a nice place for her, adding, "Rick isn't here to help and Dad won't help with these situations, so it's all up to me. I had to find you another new place because they can't take care of you at Atria anymore." Then I began crying.

Diane hates when I cry, so she came and put her arms around me and said it was okay. Then she wanted to know why Dad wouldn't help! She was fixated on and angry about that now. I tried to explain it wasn't because he didn't want to help, but he thought I was better at these things. He wasn't as strong in many ways as I was. All of this had been very hard on him. She finally agreed to the move.

I took her over to The Manse and let her walk through the place and meet all the people who worked there. I took her for a walk around the grounds so she could see how beautiful it was and see all the rabbits everywhere. I told her she could walk around the park-like yard whenever she wanted. I could tell she felt a little better after the visit.

One of the things I liked about The Manse was that Diane could wander around on her own. All the places RJ and I had visited were lockdown facilities; you had to press a code into a keypad to get outside and only the staff had it. Here, the only way in or out of the grounds was the automatic entry gate, which is closely watched. The grounds were completely surrounded by an iron fence, but because they were so large, it felt very open.

We moved her within the week. Atria was wonderful and gave us all our deposit back along with our balance of that month's rent even though I only gave them one week's notice. I think they were probably relieved we were taking her someplace where she could be more closely watched.

All of this had happened in a little over a week after our talk with Abdon. He was there to help with her transition in any way he could. I packed her suitcase and asked Abdon to pick her up Friday night for the weekend. When they were gone, I packed up all her stuff. I thought it would be easier this time if she wasn't around to see it all happen. She'd simply show up at her new home and it would all be ready for her.

Saturday, the movers moved Diane's possessions into her new home. Dad and Margie were there to help; RJ was under the weather. We worked all day, hanging her pictures and putting everything in its place, so it was quite similar to her room at Atria. It was charming, and I hoped she'd quickly feel at home.

We then asked Abdon to bring Diane to her new home, but when they arrived, she didn't want to get out of the car. She wouldn't speak to any of us; she really was angry. Dad walked up to her to give her a hug and she shunned him and walked the other way. Dad began tearing up, and I felt horrible. She'd misinterpreted what I'd said when I told her Dad wouldn't help me. She was mad at him! Diane always hugged Dad and gave him a big smile, but not today. I think she felt as though she'd been tricked. She was expecting to have Abdon take her back to her room at Atria and he brought her here instead.

Abdon, angel that he is, was always able to get Diane in a good mood. He was great about joking with her and teasing her, which she loved. Usually he could easily make her smile and laugh. Abdon walked her around and we finally left them alone so he could help her get comfortable with her new place.

I think Abdon was relieved, too. He later told me that he could now be the friend to her that he wanted to be. Without the stress of feeling responsible for watching over Diane all day long, he could concentrate more on his duties at Atria and more fully enjoy hanging out with her in his spare time. Their relationship had turned from caregiver to lover back to caregiver.

The following day I had to take Diane for a vaccination required by The Manse. On the drive over, I told her she'd really hurt Dad's feelings when she shunned him the day before. I explained again what I'd been trying to say to her the day I was convincing her she needed to move. I'd been frustrated and perhaps what I said was misinterpreted. I said Dad was there for her for most things, but there were certain things he wanted me to handle. She understood and wanted to talk to Dad. I called him from the car and put her on speakerphone so she could say she loved him.

We thought this would be when Abdon would exit the stage, but he actually found a new apartment and moved closer to The Manse. He continued to visit Diane, taking her for walks and out to dinner a few nights a week. This was love, even though it couldn't be a "normal" relationship. Abdon's feelings truly went deep, even though part of him knew he should be distancing himself from Diane to protect himself from future pain.

Abdon even planted rose bushes in front of Diane's cottage. I finally asked him about his plan to start breaking it off. He said he'd tried but he couldn't do it. He was too much in love with Diane at this point. What a lucky girl she was to have him!

The Manse was built on three acres of parkland, and Diane was free to walk around wherever she wanted. Her roommates were still pretty cognitive, much more than Diane was, and they were 72, 80, and 96! They watched over Diane and she ended up thanking me; she really liked it there and everyone was wonderful.

Abdon said, "I'd come over to visit her some nights and she'd look at me and ask if I was tired. When I said I was, she'd tell me I didn't have to come. I'd look at her and think how could I not be here?"

Diane started declining very steadily after we moved her into The Manse. The staff doctor was monitoring her, and that worried me because I'd seen so many of the residents drugged and just sitting on the sofa.

I still picked up Diane once or twice a week and spent the day with her. Dad and Margie took her out one day a week and Abdon took her out a few days. We were having lunch at Sammy's Pizza when she started hallucinating. She was sure Abdon was cheating on her with one of the ladies he worked with, and I couldn't convince her otherwise. She started looking behind us and talking about who was there. When I said no one was there, she just looked at me and said, "They are all laughing at you." "Who's laughing at me?" I asked. "They are; they're all laughing at you," she said. I tried to convince her no one was there.

I asked the staff at The Manse if they had any experiences with Diane's hallucinating around them, and they said no. They told me if I wanted to speak to a doctor, they had one I could take her to right next door. When I told him about her hallucinating, he reprimanded me for not agreeing with her! He told me just go along with everything she said, that I shouldn't upset her. He didn't think she needed any drugs and sent us on our way.

Several researchers have been working together and recently announced success in developing a drug that targets the symptoms of Alzheimer's disease in mice. They formed a drug called J147 that not only enhanced memory in normal mice but also prevented memory loss in mice with Alzheimer's.—About.com

Diane's friend Pam called to say that she, Heather, Kathy, and a bunch of other people from the TV station were having a reunion lunch and wanted Diane to be there. I told Pam that Diane had declined a bit, so be prepared. When the day came, I helped dress up Diane a little and put some makeup on her so she looked like her old self. Kathy came to drive Diane to the lunch. I noticed the reaction on her face when she saw how Diane was acting, but she was so kind and carefully put her in the car.

That was the last time any of her friends saw Diane. They were a bit shocked that she could barely speak and was quite confused. Some time later, another long-time friend, Judy, called me when she was in town visiting and asked to see Diane. I told her it was better she didn't; Diane was no longer herself and I wanted her to be remembered the way she used to be. Judy, Diane, and Pam had been the "cut-ups" at the station, and I'd heard stories of their escapades for 18 years! I know how hard it had been on Pam and Heather to see Diane, and I didn't want Judy to have to go through the same thing. Diane wouldn't have known Judy anyway, and I thought it would be too hard on her. Judy understood.

Someone from The Manse called me quite often now to discuss issues occurring with Diane. I'd heard the stories of Alzheimer's patients becoming angry, but never in a million years did I think it would happen to our sweet little Diane—until I got a call to tell me she'd taken down an older lady and sent her to the hospital. I was shocked! It turned out there was a lady who stole everything around the place and when she tried to steal Diane's purse, Diane pushed her away and she fell. The staff stood up for Diane in this case.

Dad and I laughed about this later, saying it was not like Diane, but the more I thought about it, it kind of was. She was always a little toughie and extremely strong for her petite 5'2" frame. I used to say it was the fiery red hair that was to blame. I remember when we were teenagers, if I didn't cooperate with what she wanted me to do, she'd threaten to beat me up. She slugged me pretty hard a few times. In fact, one day when Diane was probably 16, we were visiting our cousins for a holiday; we had 21 cousins in San Diego alone. One of our older cousins, John, a Robert Redford look-a-like who was very popular with the girls, probably 6' tall and well built, started teasing Diane. Before we knew it she'd taken him down to the floor and was sitting on top of him! John was teased about that for many years to come. I think Rick was a little afraid of her, too, and because he wasn't allowed to touch us girls, he was left defenseless.

One day, Dad and Margie had taken Diane to lunch and when they were in their car getting ready to leave, one of The Manse staff members asked them if they'd come back in for a minute. They were trying to give Diane her meds and she wasn't letting them. Dad said he was shocked to see Diane hitting a table and yelling that she didn't want to take the meds. He was horrified; he'd never seen her that way. I understand another time she scratched a staff member on the neck when the woman was trying to give Diane her meds, and they sedated her.

Sometime later, Abdon called to tell me that Diane seemed heavily sedated and not herself when he'd visited her the previous night. He suggested I call the staff and check into what they were giving her.

When I found out she was probably being sedated, I freaked out and called The Manse, asking how that could be done without asking my permission. They replied that when I moved her in, I'd signed something saying they were now in control of giving her whatever they thought was necessary to keep her calm and easily manageable. That broke my heart! This was the beginning of the end, I thought, no turning back now. She was going to be one of them, a zombie sitting lifeless on the sofa all day in front of a TV, either unaware or asleep.

Diane had become very confused and at times I don't think she knew who Dad and I were, which was very difficult for both of us. We knew that would occur eventually, as it does with most Alzheimer's patients, but it still sent us both home crying the first time it happened.

Rick and Trudy were coming to visit, and I'd been prompting Diane for weeks, reminding her that our brother was coming to see her. When they arrived, Diane hugged him as soon as she saw him. We were all relieved, but I think the next day she really didn't recognize him.

On March 6, 2010, Diane's 56th birthday, I picked her up to take her to Dad and Margie's for dinner. Our sister-in-law Claudia's birthday was two days after Diane's, and we usually celebrated them together. They were even the same age. When I tried to get Diane dressed and put some makeup on her, she sat down and said "NO!" This was my first experience with this behavior and I was shocked. I tried to explain that everyone was waiting for us to celebrate her birthday and she couldn't go in the dirty sweat clothes she was dressed in, but she said "NO!" again. I sat on her bed in tears, not knowing what I was going to do. She sat in her chair looking down at the floor and I just waited. After a while, she finally changed her mind and let me get her ready.

Diane sat at the dinner table in a total daze. Jack and Claudia were shocked to see her this way. The drugs she was on were changing her; she really wasn't Diane anymore. When Dad and I had a moment alone in the kitchen, I told him about the struggle I had getting her there that night and that I thought this would be her last birthday.

Abdon was still hanging in there with Diane. He probably had a stronger connection with her than anyone at this point. He was always light and cheerful with her and could still bring a smile to her face. He had a real gift for this. I think it was becoming harder and harder for Dad and me to be like Abdon when we were around her because we were so scared for her and it was just killing us to see her slip away from us so quickly now.

Dad called me one morning saying Diane had been taken to the hospital and I needed to go over there. The staff at The Manse said she had a seizure. They found her lying next to her bed foaming at the mouth and they called the paramedics. I phoned the hospital and spoke to the doctor on call in the ER. He said they were going to run a series of tests to see what may have caused the seizure and unless I heard otherwise, I could pick her up at 1 p.m.

I hate hospitals! Just walking into them creeps me out. I found Diane lying on a bed in a room with an IV in her arm; she was totally knocked out. When I asked a nurse why they had sedated her, she said Diane was screaming so loudly they had no other choice.

They took out the IV and she slowly woke up. I tried to lift her to get her dressed, but when I moved her she screamed! I laid her back down and told the nurse she'd screamed because she was hurt. The nurse said they'd run several tests and nothing showed up on any of them, implying there was nothing wrong with her. I wasn't satisfied. I said the way she'd reacted when I tried to help her up meant there was definitely something wrong with her back. I asked if they'd taken an X-ray of her back and she said they hadn't but she'd request one right away. Nothing showed up on that X-ray, but we still couldn't move her without her screaming out in pain, so she was admitted.

We were there for many hours before a room became available. Diane was put in a room with a woman who apparently was recovering from surgery. I felt bad for her because every time they moved Diane, she'd scream. They finally gave her a sedative to help her sleep and I left for the night.

I was there for the next several days and they still couldn't figure out what was wrong with Diane. They ran $10,000 worth of tests, which thank God were paid for by Medicare. The nurses told me they were convinced she was screaming because she was scared. I disagreed. "That is not the case," I said. "I know my sister better than anyone and I know how tough she can be. This isn't because she has Alzheimer's or she's scared!" I was so frustrated with them. I believe when they found out she had Alzheimer's, they just blamed her behavior on the disease and gave up looking for the real cause of her pain.

As I sat there and watched her, I noticed she was fine until I lifted her electronic bed to a certain degree, when the smile on her face would be replaced by an excruciating look of pain. I figured out her back must be "out." This comes from my own personal experience; I'd thrown out my back before and it was the most painful thing I'd ever been through. I told the doctor what I thought and asked if we could give her some muscle relaxers. It was amazing to me that no medical professional could figure this out! They were all too busy to just sit and watch her like I did.

They kept saying they were going to bring in a physical therapist. Finally on the third day, when this hadn't happened, Dad, Margie, and I started lifting Diane's legs slowly while she was lying in bed to see if she could even move them because she'd been lying around for so long. She seemed to be okay with that part, and I told her doctor I wanted to check her out of the hospital. I was afraid of the lack of attention she was getting from these people. Diane could no longer feed herself, and I told the staff they needed to help her eat each meal. However, every time I came to the hospital, there was a full tray of food they'd just left there for her.

The doctor said the physical therapists had to sign a report saying Diane was capable of walking before she could be discharged. I begged the doctor to get the therapists up there so we could get her back to The Manse. I wanted her out of there ASAP!

I was told to meet the physical therapists in her room the next day at 10 a.m. When they showed up, I explained I just wanted them to get her up and walking so I could break her out of there. They were great—the first nice people I'd met since we checked in Diane.

They first got her in a wheelchair, which caused much screaming. Then they asked me what Diane liked to do. Did she like to dance? I said she loved to dance. Does she like café mochas? I said she loves them, so down the hall we went and into the therapy room. Along the way, the female therapist bought her a café mocha and let her have a sip. Then the other therapist, who was a really cute young guy with red hair, turned on a radio and started to dance with Diane in the wheelchair, coaxing her to stand up. He was a great dancer, and before long we all started to dance. The female therapist was holding the café mocha in front of Diane to entice her to get up out of the chair. Diane smiled and danced in the wheelchair, but she didn't want to get up.

Finally, after trying this for a while and getting many strange looks from everyone else in the therapy room, the therapists put a strap around Diane's waist and lifted her out of the chair to help her walk. She was yelping a little, but we took her outside and walked her down the sidewalk, just enough for them to write up her release form.

After we took Diane back to her room, I told the doctor I had the release form signed and I wanted her to sign off as well so Diane could leave the hospital. She agreed, probably because I'd been such a pain in her side for a few days, and I called The Manse to send a van with a wheelchair to pick up Diane. They were there in no time and we got her back home that afternoon. It was a long day but we did it; we broke her out of that terrible place and now she could recover at her home, where everyone loved and cared for her. Phew!

Diane was walking again in a few days, slowly, but walking. We still didn't know what was wrong with her, but I assumed she'd strained her back and it just took some time to heal.

A few days after that, I visited Diane and we walked out to the big covered swing on the front lawn where we often sat and watched all the bunnies. A friend of mine, whose name is also Diane, had a mother with Alzheimer's. She'd told me her brother always told their mother that she was in control of her own body and mind, and she had the power to leave her body and this earth anytime she was ready.

It might have been too late for me to have this conversation with Diane, but I told her the same thing that day while we sat on the swing. She didn't respond at all. I don't really know if she understood what I was saying, but I could only hope it might sink in. I told her she didn't have to worry about Dad or me anymore. Dad had Margie and I had RJ, and we'd be fine if she left us now. It was okay if she wanted to let go.

I told Diane we totally understood that this was no life for her—being 56 years old, sitting on a sofa in diapers with a bunch of 70- to 90-year-olds, sedated all the time, totally unaware of what was happening to her. It wasn't the life any of us wanted, including her. I knew she didn't want to live like this.

Diane was always such a proud and private person and now she had to have others bath her, toilet her, feed her, brush her teeth, and dress her. When she first started needing more assistance, she was still pretty cognitive and was totally humiliated. She initially fought off the staff when they tried to help her, but soon she sunk deeper into the disease and wasn't as aware of the humiliation, which I think was a blessing.

Around this time Dad told me he wished Diane would just go to sleep one night and not wake up. Can you imagine how hard this must be for a father to say about his child? Until you see your child go through what Diane did and be in such a terrible state, it's really hard to understand. I think I made him feel better when I told him I'd been praying for that same thing for some time. As I did my beach runs, instead of praying God would heal her like I used to, I'd pray for God to take her now. She'd accomplished everything she could in this body and in this lifetime. It was time for a fresh start for her in the next world.

Not long after this, I got a call one afternoon from Dad while I was in an appointment. The Manse had called to tell him Diane had an accident and needed to go to the hospital right away. I rushed over to The Manse and found Diane with a nurse, who told me she'd stuck her hand through a fence to pet a dog, which wasn't surprising because she's a huge animal lover. She quickly pulled back her hand when the dog came running toward her and had torn open the whole top of it. I rushed her over to the emergency room of a different nearby hospital; I refused to take her to the one she'd just been in.

When we were seen, the doctor had to stick a needle in Diane's hand to numb her so he could stitch her up. She screamed bloody murder, got very angry, and hit the doctor! Thank goodness he was a big friendly guy. I had to practically sit on her to control the hitting so they could finish. Poor thing, it was awful.

I took her back in two days and because she'd torn off the bandage, the wound had become infected and turned into

MRSA, a serious staph infection. She was given antibiotics, and I had to take her back every other day for 10 days to have her hand checked. She could hardly walk at this point. Her little body was just not cooperating anymore.

Up to this point, I haven't shared a subject Diane and I had discussed the day she was diagnosed with Alzheimer's, when she was 50 years old and still very aware of what was happening to her. On our drive to my dad's house to tell him the devastating news, Diane made me promise her I'd never let her go all the way. I understood what she was saying but I didn't want to talk negatively. I told her she didn't have to worry about that because we were going to heal her!

We had this conversation again later. One day she asked if I'd put anything in writing about our discussion and I responded no; she had to write it. We had a living trust drafted when Diane was first diagnosed with Alzheimer's, and the medical portion stated that there be no heroics and that she not be kept alive by assistance. But she wanted something a little more precise, stating that she didn't want me to let her go all the way to a vegetative state with this horrible disease. This was when she told me she needed me to write something because she couldn't write well anymore or even use the computer. I kept thinking I needed to do what she asked and get her signature before she could no longer sign her name. I never did—not that it would have done any good anyway, as I came to find out.

We'd talked about this in my family; we don't want to be left in a coma, live as a vegetable, or be a burden to anyone. If we were ever in a state where we couldn't fully enjoy life, the family would make sure there were no heroics. Our directives are in our living trusts and it all sounds great on paper. However, the reality is you can't do a damn thing about it when you're in a situation like Diane's.

I'd told RJ about the conversations Diane and I had—yet here she was, in an advanced stage of Alzheimer's, sedated for most of the day, and in diapers. I'd already let her go further than she would have ever wanted to go—further than anyone would ever want to go—but there was nothing I could do.

One morning I read an article in the Sunday paper about a local couple who'd been married for around 60 years; both had been afflicted with a disease that would take their lives. Because they didn't want to suffer through long and horrible deaths, they made a decision to go to a place in Switzerland called Dignity, where they'd be able to drink a solution and go to sleep forever.

I shared that story with Lorraine, a girlfriend who's one of the editors of this book and whose mother had died of Alzheimer's. She instantly volunteered to help me get Diane to Switzerland. She understood completely after watching her mother's demise due to this horrible disease.

That night, I told RJ that Lorraine and I were taking Diane to Switzerland. It was a little in jest, but I really wanted to do this for Diane. I'd made her a promise, and I felt just horrible that I hadn't done something by now. RJ wasn't too keen on the idea; he didn't want his wife to end up in jail. As it turned out, Diane had progressed too far into the disease to get on a plane for an overseas flight anyway. I then started looking at the right to die laws in the state of Washington. Unfortunately, you have to be a resident of that state for few years before you can "take matters into your own hands."

After I told RJ that Diane had been diagnosed with MRSA, he looked at me with those big brown eyes and said if I didn't put her on the antibiotics, the infection could possibly assist in taking Diane in the direction we were hoping for. One of his dearest friends, Fred, had lost his wife a few years previously to MRSA.

She'd gone into the hospital for simple hip replacement surgery, got a staph infection while recovering, and died unexpectedly. MRSA apparently runs rampant in hospitals and is extremely difficult to control. It took Fred's wife very quickly. I was in anguish. If I'd only known! I'd already had the prescription filled and given it to the nursing staff at The Manse. It was too late. I couldn't call them and tell them to stop giving her the drugs.

I'd shared Diane's story over the years with many of my clients who were doctors, so they knew what we were facing. In what I call "joking on the square" (pretending I'm joking when really there's a bit of truth behind what I'm saying), I'd say if they'd all give me just a small amount of morphine, we could end Diane's suffering ourselves. I think deep in my heart I was hoping for the story to get out that I was in need of a "Dr. Kevorkian" and perhaps someone would volunteer, but no one ever did. I was so angry with Dr. Kevorkian for being so careless and getting arrested (and subsequently dying)!

The Accident

A few days later, I got another call from The Manse. They'd just sent Diane to the hospital in an ambulance because when they went to wake her up, they found her lying on the floor again and foaming at the mouth; they thought she might have had another seizure. I'd informed The Manse never to send her back to that same hospital, but they did.

The hospital ran another $10,000 worth of tests and found nothing, so they said we could take Diane home. I asked my dad to pick her up because I had an appointment with a client; I'd check in on her later in the day.

Dad called me a little later and said the hospital had just called him to tell him he couldn't take Diane home because she had a broken hip! Dad said I needed to call right away and talk to the surgeon. I was furious! I called The Manse first and asked if her hip was broken when they sent her off in the ambulance. They said no; she'd walked over to the ambulance. She didn't have a broken hip when she went in! Did the hospital staff drop her? How the hell did she get a broken hip? I was out for blood, and I called the surgeon who was assisting Diane. As soon as he said he wanted to do hip replacement surgery right away, I broke into tears and said, "She can't go through this! I can't put her through this!" That surgeon turned out to be angel, because he stopped and said, "You don't have to. We can call in hospice."

Had God answered my prayers? As I already mentioned, I'd recently changed my prayers from please heal Diane to please take her now, take her away from this horrible suffering. I'd been asking for this new outcome for many months when I had the surprising phone conversation with the surgeon. It wasn't until I hung up that I realized he was granting us the wish for Diane I'd been praying for.

Until the doctor explained it to me, I really hadn't known what hospice was. I still didn't thoroughly understand what was to take place, so I called Dad. I told him what the surgeon suggested as an alternative to hip replacement surgery because he agreed with me that Diane wasn't a candidate for it. Dad and I cried together but then agreed this was the right thing to do. I called Rick, and he and Trudy also agreed with the decision. Thus, with the family's blessing, this surgeon, this guardian angel who I never got to meet, wrote up the necessary paperwork and set the wheels in motion for Diane to go into hospice.

The surgeon told me I had to select the hospice we wanted to use and let him know; he'd make the necessary arrangements and get the paperwork started. I immediately called my client Stephanie Wilde-Heywood, who's a nurse, and asked for help finding a hospice. She said she'd talk to her husband, Tom Heywood, the heart surgeon I mentioned earlier, and get right back to me. Within minutes, Stephanie called back and said they recommended VISTAS. By this time I couldn't even talk, I was crying so hard. I could feel Stephanie's arms reaching through the phone lines and giving me a huge hug. For years she'd been supporting me throughout this whole ordeal with Diane. Years later, her mother, another long-time client of mine, also was afflicted with Alzheimer's disease.

I was in shock and just headed over to the hospital. I called RJ when I had a moment of sanity and told him I was coming to pick him up at work because I needed him to be with me for support. RJ had gone through hospice with his parents, both of whom died of cancer. He'd told me many times it's a horribly difficult thing to experience, but now that we had the opportunity, I was determined to release Diane from her body as I'd promised her I would.

We arrived at the hospital and the hospice people were there with loads of paperwork. Thank goodness I brought RJ along. I was a total mess and wasn't able to really comprehend anything at this point. Because I had Diane's power of attorney, I was in charge of everything in her life and I was able to sign all the papers.

Afterward we checked on Diane. She gave me a big smile, not because she really knew I was her sister, but because I looked like someone she knew and liked. That was the last time I ever saw my sister awake.

The hospice people told us that we had to find a nursing home for Diane. One of the hospice nurses said she wasn't supposed to give out recommendations, but she felt sorry for me because I had no idea where to start looking and this had to happen pretty quickly. I was quite distressed. She gave me the name of a place near our house and told me to run over there immediately because they were usually pretty full and I'd do much better in person than by just making a phone call.

I drove over to the facility and realized I'd passed it many times and had never paid much attention to the building. I walked into a beautiful lobby, up to the front desk, and told the receptionists I needed to have a room right away for my sister. I was quite demanding and then broke into tears. They said they didn't know if they could get her in right away. I persisted, saying she absolutely had to get a room that day. The receptionist got on the phone, chatted with someone for a minute, and then said, "Irene will take care of you." That made me cry even harder. My mom's name was Irene, and I had this overwhelming feeling she was here helping me through this.

We got Diane into a room the next day and they started the morphine drip. I still didn't really understand what we were doing. The surgeon had explained that she'd be on a morphine drip so she wouldn't feel any pain from the broken hip and her body would eventually give up and shut down. I assumed this had something to do with the amount of morphine they'd give her. When they told me they'd stop feeding her, I was shocked! My husband told me I'd signed all the papers saying I understood, but I was so upset and couldn't read much through my tears. I was probably only half listening, and I trusted him to know what to do since he'd been through it twice and he knew my wishes.

I hadn't discovered the no-feeding fact until the following day. Abdon had been there the first night to see her, bringing her ice cream. The next morning the hospice nurse told me about it and I asked her if Diane woke up and ate any. The nurse explained that Diane would no longer be awake and couldn't eat anything anyway, but she didn't have the heart to tell Abdon he couldn't try and give her the ice cream. When I asked her what she meant, she explained Diane would no longer be fed and that's what would make her body shut down, not the morphine! They were giving her enough morphine to put her in a comatose state so she'd never wake up, but she was basically being starved to death. I was horrified at what we were doing to her.

When animals are sick and you know they're not going to make it, you're encouraged to do the humane thing and let them go easily without any more suffering. You're able to give them a shot and let them go onto the next life peacefully. Why isn't that allowed for humans—for our loved ones?

The next day I walked into Diane's room to sit with her, and I was told I needed to sign some more papers. When I arrived at the desk, Irene was waiting for me—my next-door neighbor Irene, the only other Irene I'd ever met! What are the chances that she was the one who got Diane into the facility and was taking care of her? She didn't know Diane was my sister, and she was just as shocked as I was!

Poor Abdon. When he got off work that night, he met me there along with Dad and Margie. We all sat in the dining room to talk. I'd filled out a lot of the paperwork incorrectly and was in the dining room redoing it. At a time like this, it is very difficult to concentrate on what seem to be such mundane, unimportant questions.

Abdon wasn't accepting what we were doing very well. He told me later he was very angry with us. We cried together and I explained to Abdon the pact I'd made with Diane. I knew he loved her but she'd made me promise I wouldn't let her live this way. He said he understood, but I don't really think he could.

Abdon had never known the Diane we did—the funny, light-hearted jokester we'd all known and loved. He only knew her with Alzheimer's, and he loved her too much to let her go. He later admitted this to me: "I was much more selfish than you were. I didn't care. I just was scared and more concerned about what I wanted than what she needed. As much as it hurt to accept your choice, I knew it was the right one. And if I really loved her the way I said I did, I'd have to accept it, but it really hurt me to know she wasn't going to be around anymore."

Abdon also had a lot more to say: "I used to resent you and your dad a little because you guys didn't visit Diane as much at the end, but then I had to put myself in your place. How would I like it if my son was in this same situation and how would I feel about seeing him every day and watching him decline the way you had to watch Diane decline over the last six years. It was a fight back and forth and yes I did resent you, but I knew why you did it. I really admired you for your strength.

"I was really mad at myself for not being able to do more for her. I was mad at the world, I was mad at God. I used to say, hey, there are some really mean people out there. Why doesn't this happen to them instead of her! I didn't have to know her long to realize she was such a nice person, such a beautiful person. All you had to do was look into her eyes. I didn't have to know her past. I only had to know the present and our time together."

I sat with Diane for several hours a day, watching her and talking to her. Even though she was in a coma because of the morphine, I thought she could still hear me and know I was there for her.

One day I thought I'd give her a manicure and pedicure because her fingernails were really long and one of the girls at The Manse had painted them purple. She looked a bit like Morticia Addams. I used to take Diane in for a manicure and pedicure at least once a month. She'd loved it except when they massaged her feet, which were extremely ticklish; they had a hard time holding onto them. Diane would sit in the chair and just giggle. On this day, I did her hands first and when I got to the feet, even though she was highly sedated, her feet twitched when I touched them. I had to chuckle; she was still in there, hanging out with me.

I had to go back to The Manse to clear out Diane's room because it was almost the end of the month. Dad and Margie met me there. We looked through Diane's photo albums for hours, reminiscing. Then, I once again filled up my car with all of Diane's personal belongings, which I donated. I decided I couldn't deal with all her furniture, so I left the room exactly as it was and told the owner of The Manse it was our gift to them for helping us with Diane.

I thought because Diane had been so thin to begin with, she'd probably be with us only a few more days, but she kept hanging onto this life. One of her doctors, a very beautiful and spiritual woman, came in one day and asked if there might be someone Diane was waiting to say goodbye to. I immediately thought, "Oh my God, she's waiting for Rick to get here!" I'd been in touch with Rick and Trudy and they were standing by in Hawaii.

I told Trudy the doctor recommended that Rick call Diane and talk to her. When he got off work, we set up a time for the call. I put him on speaker and put the phone up to her ear. My brother is not one who's ever shared his feelings with me, so I was quite surprised by the beautiful things he said to her. He told her he loved her and it was okay if she left us now; it was time she went to see Mom and all our other family and friends who'd already passed. He told her they were all waiting for her and we'd all be okay. We both cried and I told him I'd be in touch.

I think after that, Rick understood what I was going through, and he and Trudy decided to hop on a plane to come help me. After they arrived, Rick and Trudy, Dad and Margie, and RJ and I took shifts, staying with Diane for 10 long days. She never regained consciousness, but we talked to her constantly, mostly telling her how much we loved her and it was okay to leave us now; we would all be fine.

I hadn't been to a funeral in probably 25 years. I went to two besides my mother's when I was 19 and swore I'd never go to another one again. Diane and I had talked about the funeral for our mom's father, our grandfather. Grandpa was a grumpy old curmudgeon tightwad! He was mean to everyone and a pretty miserable old man in general. When we were teenagers he would only give us a dollar for Christmas and birthdays, even though he had plenty of money. He didn't treat my mother well because I guess she was the black sheep of the family and, from what I heard, a little rebellious.

My mom told us that she never remembered her dad ever picking her up and putting her on his lap or ever holding her. She told me a story that always stuck with me. After my grandma died, all my mom's siblings tried to let my grandpa live with them, except my mom; she wouldn't. When finally no one could stand having him around anymore, they put him in a retirement home. Mom would pick him up once a week and take him out to do his errands. She said one day she took him to the bank to deposit his monthly check from the farm he still owned back in North Dakota. He deposited a large amount of money into his account and afterward asked my mom if she'd like to stop to have a cup of coffee before heading back. They went to Denny's and she ordered a cup of coffee and a dessert. He said very coldly, "I said I'd buy you a cup of coffee, not a dessert."

At my grandfather's funeral, Diane and I were sitting in the front row. The minister giving the eulogy was from our church, but he'd never met my grandfather because he never attended services. He started out by saying something about our grandfather being a kind and generous person. Diane looked over at me and made this face with big eyes like "what?" We both tried so hard not to burst out laughing. Our eyes filled up with tears from this effort, but everyone thought they were tears of sorrow.

Diane and I would sometimes talk about what we wanted when we left this world: a big Irish wake. We wanted to have a party that had dancing, music, and great food—a real celebration! Rick, Trudy, and I, while sitting with Diane as the life ebbed out of her, started talking about her Celebration of Life. By this time, I'd pretty much thought it all through and was discussing the details when I suddenly stopped. I looked at Diane and said we had to stop planning in front of her or she'd never leave—she'd want to stay for the party!

We then turned around the conversation, telling her she had a great party waiting for her, put on by friends and family she hadn't seen in years. It was time for her to go to her own party! The party we were planning was for the ones she was leaving behind, and I knew she'd be there in spirit.

The hospice nurses are the most amazing angels I met on this journey. You definitely must be a very special person to do that job. I'd sit for hours with these women and ask them about what gave them the strength to do it. I remember one nurse said she thinks it's a privilege to be able to assist someone into the next life and make it as painless and peaceful as possible.

The hospice nurses were by Diane's side almost 24/7, even though the facility she was in had its own nurses. The hospice nurses wanted to be there, watching her all the time. What a sense of comfort for our family, knowing someone was always watching over Diane. The hospice nurses monitored the morphine drip. If the facility nurses moved Diane while bathing her, for instance, and she felt anything, they increased the dose to make sure she was comfortable. I got to know one nurse who'd been there several days. She told me she used to have a chocolate store and made candies. I told her Diane would have loved her! She couldn't go a day without chocolate. When she told me the name of her shop was Serendipity, it seemed absolutely appropriate. Remember the one thing on Diane's list to do when we were in New York was go to Serendipity, the "dessert shop" she'd seen in a movie.

During one of my days sitting with Diane, it dawned on me that I needed to call UCSD to tell them about her situation, because she wanted to donate her body to research. I reached someone right away, but was shocked to learn they couldn't accept the donation because she wasn't involved in a research study. I thought because we'd seen doctors at UCSD, Diane would be a candidate; however, because she was living on her own during that time, she wasn't able to participate in any study that involved being on drugs. Only those with constant supervision could be in those studies.

I then called the National Network of Organ Donors, because Diane had noted that she wanted to be a donor on her driver's license, but it couldn't take her, either! Its researchers were still unsure of how Alzheimer's disease affects body tissue.

I sat there at my desk in shock. This isn't happening! Diane wanted to donate her body to science. This can't all be for naught!

Within an hour, my mood changed appreciably, as my angels were working for me yet again. I received a call from Jacopo Annese, Ph.D., director of the Brain Observatory. UCSD and the National Network of Organ

Donors had shared my story with him. He gave me some information about his research company and asked me to check out his website. He said he'd be honored to take Diane's brain for research.

I immediately visited his website and, after learning more about his cause, I called Dad and then Rick and Trudy to tell them what I wanted to do. With them on board, I called Jacopo back and agreed to donate Diane's brain to his research company. He was so sweet and caring; there was an immediate connection. We spoke a few times that week so I could give him reports on Diane's condition. He told me to call him as soon as she'd passed.

Independence Day

The hospice nurse told us Diane would be passing very soon; she could tell by the color of the skin on her hands. We all sat with her for hours. We cried and waited and cried and waited. Finally, late that evening, RJ said we should leave because she was probably waiting for our departure so we wouldn't have to see her go. I looked at the clock every hour that night as I lay in bed, waiting for the phone to ring. Finally, at 7 a.m. on July 4, 2010, Irene called to tell me she had bad news. I told her, no Irene, it's not bad news; it's good news, thank you.

Diane found her independence from Alzheimer's disease on the Fourth of July. How appropriate. I called the family and Abdon and told them to plan to come over. I called Jacopo Annese. I apologized for putting a damper on his holiday celebration and he replied, "It's fine. I'm Italian so I really don't celebrate July 4th."

We had a barbecue at our house that day, something we'd already planned for the family. We cried and talked about

Diane all day. We told lots of stories and when it got dark, we walked to the park next door with our chairs and blankets and watched the fireworks show. What a wonderful sendoff for my beloved sister.

The next day we worked on the details of Diane's party. We went through our photo albums and found pictures of her doing all the fun things that made up her life: many of the funny faces she always made; flipping me off; jumping out of a plane; driving a motorcycle; posing with a few of the famous people she met while working at the TV station, such as Betty White and Harry Smith; and smiling with her animals. We put the photos on two large poster boards and displayed them on easels so people could look at them at her farewell party. Our dear friend Edgar put together a slide show featuring those great images, complete with music, which would play on a big screen TV during the celebration.

Diane's Celebration of Life was held in Jack and Claudia's backyard, where RJ and I got married, where they got married, and where their son, Brian, got married. We joked that we just needed to have one more marriage there and it would be "Four Weddings and a Funeral."

It was a beautiful day. We served Mexican food because that was Diane's favorite. We drank margaritas. We had chocolate cake and ice cream because no day was complete in Diane's life without those treats. Margie made her famous lemon meringue pies.

Sixty-two people from many different stages of Diane's life attended. Her friends from Pearson Ford and the TV station came, as did her old neighbors and many of our relatives I hadn't seen in years—and all my girlfriends showed up for me. I asked that this be a joyous occasion and explained that Diane always wanted an Irish wake, and that's what we were trying to do (despite the Mexican food!). We wanted people to share stories about Diane's sense of humor, because that and her quick wit were truly her blessings, and that's how we wanted to remember her.

Many people stood up and told funny stories about Diane and how she made them laugh. Abdon appeared late and was unaware of the story about the Irish wake. He was holding a dozen red roses. I asked him if he wanted to say anything and to my surprise he took the microphone and talked for quite a while. He broke everyone's heart by telling their story and how lucky he felt to have been able to spend that last year and half with her. He said she taught him how to really love. There was not a dry eye in the place. Abdon was truly an angel. He repeated what he'd said to me before: He was lucky to meet her when he did because if they'd met prior to her illness, she probably wouldn't have been interested in him.

After everyone who wanted to speak had finished, we enjoyed the food, drank, and finally celebrated some more by playing rock 'n' roll music and dancing, because that was what Diane loved. It was the Irish wake, the big party she'd always talked about having! I think she had a good time.

While you might think this is the end of the story, there is one more chapter.

The Brain Observatory

Jacopo picked up Diane soon after I called him that July 4th morning and, after taking an MRI, removed her brain. With his connections he was able to have UCSD pick up her body after all, and it was donated for research just as she'd requested. I later got a letter from the National Network of Organ Donors informing me that it was able to use her eye tissue as well. Ultimately, her body was cremated and her ashes were scattered at sea, also as she would have wanted. This was okay with me because I have a very strong belief that once you die, your soul has left your body. Diane's body had no meaning to me now, but it was very valuable to the researchers.

The work with Jacopo was just starting. When he found out I'd documented everything about Diane's six years with Alzheimer's, he was ecstatic! Jacopo was looking for a brain with a story. He told me he wanted not only to study Diane's brain but also to learn everything about her. He wanted to know her likes and dislikes, what she loved to do, what her favorite food was, and all about her personality; he wanted to get to know Diane, not just her brain. He told me the first time I talked to him that Diane would never be just a specimen to him. Jacopo told me to give him a call when I was ready to talk. I cried every day for weeks after Diane left us, and it took me several more weeks before I reached the point where I thought I could talk about her.

When I did go to meet Jacopo, I brought a picture of Diane with me because I felt he should have a visual of her. He immediately downloaded it onto his computer, and then called the staff over and said, "Here is our Diane." Everyone said ahhhh.

Jacopo walked me though the lab and showed me the whole process. He pulled out Diane's Alzheimer's safe return ID bracelet from his desk, explaining he felt a connection with it because when he was a child his mother made him wear one like it in case he got lost. He asked if I wanted it, and I said no; it was too painful.

Jacopo showed me the MRI he'd taken of Diane's brain and compared it to a healthy brain, which happened to be Jacopo's mother's. It was amazing to see how Diane's brain had shrunk an inch or so away from her skull and his healthy elderly mother's brain was almost touching the skull. You could see dark spots on Diane's brain representing the areas where it had stopped functioning.

Jacopo became well known for receiving the brain of the very famous person who'd been known as the man with the 20-second memory. He's been on Nova with that story. This man had seizures his entire life and when he was about 20, the doctors decided to try to cure the seizures with an operation that didn't go well and left him with a memory of only 20 seconds. He was studied for over 60 years until he died in his 80s, when Jacopo was selected to receive his brain for research.

I really liked Jacopo because of the way he shared information. He dissected Diane's brain into 2,600 to 3,000 slices, each the thickness of a human hair, and put each one between sheets of glass. Each slice can be blown up on a large screen and studied by scientists all over the world, giving them all the opportunity to help find a cure for this horrible disease!

Jacopo and I have worked together for a year and a half. I shared all Diane's MRIs, PET scans, and neurological studies, basically everything I'd documented over her six-year battle. We're now putting her story together, something that included hours of recorded interviews focused on Diane.

I've also done some more public interviews, with several reporters who are interested in Jacopo's work and Diane's story and with a KPBS reporter whose segment has been on TV and radio. One of my clients said she heard me on the radio.

It makes me feel so good that Diane's story is continuing; even though she's left us, she's still helping doctors all over the world study Alzheimer's and work to find a cure for the next generation. We hope they won't have to experience what she and the rest of us had to go through.

Jacopo is leaving no stone unturned, and he wants to do an MRI on my brain to compare it to Diane's. I said I'd do it as long he adheres to one condition: I don't want to be told if he sees any sign of Alzheimer's.

I recently got an email from Michael from our early-onset support group. He wanted to let me know that Mary (who'd done the Ceregene study) had passed on. She'd been admitted into a senior home and within a few weeks had a blood clot in the brain that ended her life. I guess we'll never know for sure how the Ceregene surgery would have affected her Alzheimer's over the long term. I do think she was lucky she didn't have to go "all the way."

Michael told me his wife, Peggy, is still sitting in a home. She can't really walk or talk and doesn't know him anymore. The way I see it, she's one of the unlucky ones (as is he).

Abdon and I talk frequently. He called me one day and asked if I had Diane's ID bracelet. I said no but I could get it from Jacopo. He said he really wanted it, so I called Jacopo and asked him to send it to me. When Abdon came to get it, he asked me to put it on him. I was surprised: "You want to wear it?" He replied, "Why do you think I wanted it?" As I was putting it on him, I warned him that he wouldn't be able to get it off by himself; he'd have to have someone else do it. That didn't faze him. Maybe he wore it because he was a Marine; I know a lot of people wear the "dog tags" of their fallen loved ones.

Abdon had just walked the Alzheimer's Charity Walk in Diane's name. He misses her terribly, as I do, and whenever we get together we always tell stories about her and cry together. As I write this, it's been over two and a half years, but the pain is still very sharp. He told me one day he was angry with me. I said I understood, but I'd made a promise to Diane. He replied, "No, I'm not angry about how it ended. I'm angry that you brought her into Atria that day and into my life in the first place. If it wasn't for you, I wouldn't be hurting so badly now." He laughed afterward, but I knew to a certain extent, he was joking on the square.

Karen, one of his friends who worked at the front desk at Atria and knew Diane and me, once told Abdon that whenever he sees a butterfly, it will be Diane's sprit watching over him. He says he sees butterflies often. Abdon keeps Diane's picture on the dashboard of his bus, so she still rides with him every day.

On May 15, 2012, the Obama Administration announced the release of the "Draft National Plan to Address Alzheimer's Disease." A positive step toward our nation's first ever strategic plan for Alzheimer's, this draft plan presents a comprehensive approach toward beginning to address quality care, family and caregiver support and the development of new treatments. They are setting the clock ticking toward a deadline of 2025 to finally find effective ways to treat, or at least stall, the mind-destroying disease.

I got a call from Diane's friend Heather, who now lives in her house. Her aunt had just been diagnosed with Alzheimer's and she wanted to talk about what to do next. She also told me that the mother of another of their friends, Pam, had just been diagnosed, too. I told them both I really wish this book was already published so I could give them each a copy. I only hope it will give a little insight to those having to deal with this issue.

Every 58 seconds another person in the U.S. is diagnosed with Alzheimer's disease.—Alz.org

Hope remains for the future, but for now there is no magic pill for Alzheimer's. Science needs to prevent and cure the disease. This book is a story for the families who face this disease, because there is no manual about how to deal with everything that's going to happen if this tragedy strikes someone you love.

My main reason for writing this book was initially limited to bringing awareness to Alzheimer's disease, but it expanded to address the fact that California doesn't have the "right to die law" some other states already have in place. My hope is to take a percentage of the proceeds from this book to put toward the fight to get this humane law passed, not only for those whose lives are destroyed by this disease but also for the families whose lives are devastated by it.

I didn't get the happy ending I was originally praying for when I started this book eight years ago, but the one I got works for me.

Epilogue

One day when I was with Diane in Dr. Drummen's office, he said he didn't think we could recover what she'd lost, but he had great hopes we could keep her right where she was for the rest of her life. Diane looked at me with a very worried expression on her face and said, "Does that mean if they heal me, I have to go back to work?" My heart sunk. She was afraid to get well because she didn't want to have to work again!

As I mentioned to begin this story, one reason I decided to write this book as a way to ensure Diane wouldn't have to worry about working, but she could still get well. She needed to have the desire and passion to get well or none of this was going to work. I told her that her only job was to get well and leave the rest to me. I said, "Everyone loves a happy ending, so you concentrate on giving me the happy ending this book needs to sell. That is your only job!"

I told her if she got well, the book would be a New York Times bestseller and we would be on Oprah. She said I had to do all the talking if we went on TV, and I smiled and assured her that would not be a problem. I began this book soon after, and started documenting everything we were doing so others could learn what we'd done to cure Diane. In April 2013, as I had finished my final of many edits and was getting ready to meet my publisher for the first time, I had a most unexpected development in my life. I was diagnosed with stage one breast cancer and was told that because of the position of the two tumors I had to have a mastectomy.

I was in shock. I thought I did everything right—eat well, run, use all natural products in my household, think only positive thoughts—but it turns out I was just a statistic. It was very interesting that the week before, I was out celebrating a birthday with eight of my girlfriends when my dear friend Kim told us that her mom, who calls me her adopted daughter, was just diagnosed with breast cancer. I made a toast to all of us saying we were all so blessed that the statistics are 1 in 8 women will get breast cancer and none of us had been struck with it. I don't think I knocked on wood, however, as I was saying it. When I told Kim, she jokingly socked me in the arm and said, "Thanks for taking one for the team Renae!" We both laughed.

After nine days of grueling tests, I was given a surgery date that left me only two weeks to get everything in my life in order. The week I was diagnosed, I got four new interior design jobs, and it was crazy trying to get everything in order so I could take a couple of weeks off. I was bombarded with phone calls from four of my girlfriends who had been going through stage four breast cancer for the past three years and were all still battling it. They assured me that everything would be fine and warned me about what I would be going through. One friend had warned me that

I would need to be strong for my family members because some of them will not take this well and I would find great strength within myself to make them feel better. It was true. RJ tried to be my rock, but he took the news very badly because he had lost both of his parents too young to cancer and he was very scared for me. I caught him several times tearing up and I had to comfort him. I didn't want to tell my dad until I knew exactly what was going to happen because he has still not recovered from losing Diane and I did not want to scare him. Over the past several years, whenever I talk about Diane and the book or Diane and the study with the Brain Observatory, he tears up and cannot discuss it, so I was really dreading the call to him. When all the tests were in and I knew what the procedures would be, I called him and Margie, and as I expected, he broke down on the phone. I tried so hard to be strong for him, but it is so difficult to see or hear your dad cry.

The surgery went very well. The doctors got all the cancer and I did not have to go through radiation or chemotherapy, so I was ecstatic! One of my girlfriends, Karen, organized all my friends and neighbors to bring us dinner nine nights in a row so RJ did not have to worry about meals. Jodi called to see when I was able to have a glass of wine and when I told her I was going off my pain killers in a couple of days she organized seven of my girlfriends to show up with champagne and sushi to celebrate the good news.

We ate, drank, and laughed for hours and as they say, laughter is the best medicine. It has been three weeks and I am feeling great and ready to get this book published.

I remember earlier in the book I mentioned I used to tell people who would complain about things that I thought were trivial, "If you don't have cancer or you don't have Alzheimer's, you have nothing to complain about." I still don't feel I have anything to complain about. I had a minor bump in the road and I will be fine compared to my other friends that are still battling breast cancer. I am sure there is some message that this experience was supposed to teach me and I am being very open to that.

It is now May and our friend Steve asked us the other night to his Fourth of July party. It always makes me tear up when I hear about the upcoming holiday. It will be three years this Fourth of July that Diane found her independence from Alzheimer's, and in some way I was granted independence from the disease as well. The first year I turned down all invitations to celebrate with friends because I was just too sad, but last year I decided that I needed to celebrate her on this day instead of mourn. When I see the fireworks now, I think they are for her and she is watching them with me, as she did for most of our lives.

I can't say that it has become any easier after three years; it hasn't. I still think about her and miss her every day. She comes to me in my dreams at least once a week. Sometimes she is just hanging out with me on one of our great adventures and sometimes she has Alzheimer's, but she is always her playful self and I often wake up in tears in hopes that it was not a dream.

What I can tell you and what I have learned through this process is that you can, as Abdon proved to us, love someone who is not complete. There is life after losing a loved one. You have to let yourself grieve completely and no one can tell you how long that should be—it could be years or it could be forever—but life does go on.

All we can do as family members for those who have Alzheimer's is to be there for them, do everything we can to keep them happy, and make their lives meaningful. Make sure you and your loved one become involved in your local

Alzheimer's support groups; they helped us so much. Keep up the good fight to cure this terrible disease that is taking our family members from us.

Although my life will never be the same, it is an ever-changing life bringing me lessons that I must learn from every day. I only hope that by reading this book, you will find in some small way that it makes your life a little easier while dealing with some of the same issues I have had to address.

Live every day to the fullest! That means a lot more to me now.

Acknowledgments

I dedicate this book to my husband, Richard Pommer, who stood next to me through the last few years of my sister Diane's battle and helped me make all the really hard decisions. I would have been lost without his guidance, love, and support. I thank him for suggesting that I take time away from my interior design business to finish this book and get it out to the public. I love you very much, RJ.

I also thank my dad, Bud Farley, who was by my side for seven years, helping with Diane in any way he could— mentally, physically, and financially. I love you, Dad. And thank you to Margie, his new bride, who was there helping him through the last few years of this painful ordeal and giving him great strength.

And thank you to Abdon Meraz for loving Diane and being there for her and me in so many ways. You are such an angel and I love you for all you did for her.

I also extend my gratitude to the wonderful people who helped craft my words into print. My dear friend Lorraine Alexander asked if she could edit the first manuscript for me. Lorraine knows me well, she knew Diane, and she also experienced dementia with her mother. Adrienne Moch provided her editing skills, and Kathryn Cloward and the delightful Kandon Publishing team believed in the value of sharing this story with the world.

I also thank you, the reader, for reading this book. Although Diane's story is unique, many people are journeying through similar life experiences, and I am thankful you chose to read this book. I hope it is helpful and healing.

And of course, I must thank my dear sister, Diane. This is her story, and interwoven in it is also mine. I am thankful for the graciousness Diane extended to me in being the voice of her journey. I will never forget how excited she was the day I told her that I was going to write her story. I told her that her only job was to get well because all we need is a happy ending.

About the Author

Renae Farley is an interior designer and has spent the last 30 years creating beautiful environments for her clients. She lives in San Diego, California and is passionate about running, gardening, traveling with her husband RJ, and spending time with family and friends.
www.RenaeFarley.com

Made in the USA
Las Vegas, NV
20 September 2022